Charles E. Stickney

A History of the Minisink Region

which includes the present towns of Minisink, Deerpark, Mount Hope, Greenville,

and Wawayanda in Orange County, New York - from their organization and first

settlement to their present time

Charles E. Stickney

A History of the Minisink Region
which includes the present towns of Minisink, Deerpark, Mount Hope, Greenville, and Wawayanda in Orange County, New York - from their organization and first settlement to their present time

ISBN/EAN: 9783337287818

Printed in Europe, USA, Canada, Australia, Japan

Cover: Foto ©Andreas Hilbeck / pixelio.de

More available books at **www.hansebooks.com**

A HISTORY OF THE MINISINK REGION.

A HISTORY

OF THE

MINISINK REGION:

WHICH INCLUDES THE PRESENT TOWNS OF

MINISINK, DEERPARK, MOUNT HOPE, GREEN-
VILLE AND WAWAYANDA,

IN ORANGE COUNTY, NEW YORK,

FROM THEIR ORGANIZATION AND FIRST SETTLEMENT TO THE PRESENT TIME;.

ALSO, INCLUDING

A GENERAL HISTORY OF THE FIRST SETTLEMENT
· OF THE COUNTY.

BY
CHARLES E. STICKNEY.

"This is my own, my native land!"

MIDDLETOWN, N. Y.:
COE FINCH AND I. F. GUIWITS, PUBLISHERS.
1867.

Coe Finch, Printer. Middletown, N. Y.

PREFATORY REMARKS.

READER: Before you commence the perusal of the following History, allow me to say that, if you wish to avoid disappointment, you will please bear in mind that it has not been written with the object of presenting to your view a brilliant piece of composition, or of absorbing your attention with the interest of a fascinating romance. No deep-laid plot of mystery or ideal love pervades its pages to lure you on from line to line—from beginning to end. It has been intended rather as a true record of past events—of statistics connected therewith—of old traditions that have survived the touch of time,—and in short, of the records and incidents that go towards forming a HISTORY OF THE MINISINK REGION, the first-settled portion of Orange County. To many these will prove of barren interest; and I deem it proper to say to you that this work has been written more for the purpose of supplying a void in our local history—more to preserve the details (now fast sinking into oblivion) of our ancestors' struggles with labor and inconvenience, coupled with the wiles of a savage foe, while rearing their humble cabins, when—

"His echoing axe the settler swung,"

in the wilderness two centuries ago;—more to review their actions and remember their deeds and sufferings in the glorious war of the Revolution, and their prosperity since—than to please the idle fancy for a moment, and then be thrown aside forgotten.

It is intended as a book useful for reference to the scholar—to those who like to sit by the fireside of an evening and review the doings of the olden time; and as a foundation perhaps for some future historian to build an abler work upon. If it shall accomplish but a part of this, my labor will have been rewarded.

And, reader, if it should gain your approval by furnishing needed information, or by causing some weary hour to glide smoothly away; if, when the dark hours that visit all of us are upon you—when disappointments, and troubles, and treacherous friends, enshroud your path, and you wish to banish gloomy thoughts—if, then, the comparison of your petty grievances with the gigantic ones overcome by the energy and perseverance of our forefathers, when miles separated neighbors and friends, when the war-whoop of the merciless Indian blended of an evening with the dreary howl of the wolf, and when, if a father left his home in the morning he knew not but his return at night might find it a smoldering ruin, and his wife and children mangled corpses or in a cruel captivity; if this comparison shall inspire you with new courage to contend in the "world's great din of battle,"—pleased shall I be to record you upon my list of friends, and feel thankful for the time spent in placing the narration before you.

I make no apology for the simplicity of language that clothes the incidents narrated. I am aware that many will think themselves better informed in matters of early history, and perhaps far better able to dispose of the task of preparing them for publication, than myself. But until they avail themselves of their knowledge and talents, and *do better*, I shall present my humble work for your consideration, hoping it may find what appreciation its merit deserves.

THE AUTHOR.

Slate Hill, N. Y., 1867.

CONTENTS.

A HISTORY OF THE MINISINK REGION.

CHAPTER I.

ORIGIN OF THE NAME, AND FIRST RECORDED VISIT OF A WHITE MAN.

To arrive at a proper commencing point in the history of the localities included in the limits of the region formerly known as the Minisink, it will be necessary to look back to the time when the hard-headed Peter Stuyvesant bore rule over his mimic kingdom of the New Netherlands, and sat in rigid state among the few rude habitations lying in peaceful serenity at the mouth of the Hudson—since grown in countless numbers and regal splendor, as the proud city of New York ; to the time when John Rising, Governor of the Colony of Swedes at the mouth of the Delaware, was taking upon himself a degree of importance that interfered sadly with the plans of the worthy Peter, and threatened to shipwreck his fondest hopes of conquest in that quarter. His windy manifesto, full of big Dutch words long drawn out by his valiant secretary, declaring the aforesaid Colony of New Sweden to be within the limits of his

majesty's dominions, and threatening the direst vengeance upon all who refused to acknowledge the same,
was received in scornful silence by the imperturbable
John. The insult, of itself, was bad enough, but that
so much good Dutch grammar should be absolutely
thrown away, was not to be tolerated. Days were spent
by Peter in determining a plan of revenge that would
at once avenge the slight, and maintain his dignity; and
at last the tobacco used in these deliberations resolved
itself into something more than ephemeral smoke, for it
brought an idea into the head of its august user. Other
men had covered themselves with unfading laurels on
the battle-field, why should not he ?

The consent of the mother country was first to be
obtained, for the commencement of a quarrel between
even so insignificant belligerents as these, might result
in serious complications in the home countries of Europe.
The old maps of the New Netherland provinces, made
years before by Captain Hendrickson, were brought
before the Government of Holland by Peter; the right
of Holland to the territory called New Sweden thereby
made clear, and Peter's request was granted; and he has
been handed down to posterity by the great historian
as the immortal conqueror of Fort Christina and the
Swedes. It is upon the maps thus made use of by
Peter, that the first allusion is made in history to the
old territory of Minisink. The whole of that territory
is there described as being occupied by a tribe of Indians known as the Minquas, (Vol. I. Documents relating
to the History of New York,) and this we may properly
regard as the original word from which the name Minisink was derived. At all events, this was the name by
which the Indians were known throughout that region,
till at last the Swedes and the Hollanders, with their

resolute chieftains, all fell into subjection to the mighty power of England, in 1664. Then everything underwent an entire change. The little Dutch village of New Amsterdam or Manhattan, that had been growing so quietly amid its cabbage gardens, and so unobserved in the shadow of the smoke that arose from the pipes of its steady burghers, was at once given a more sounding title, in honor of the Duke of York, and of York in England, and came out with a grand flourish as the City of New York. The little stockaded fort, and its surroundings of steep-roofed houses with their "gable ends" to the street, that had long been regarded as one of the outposts on the limits of creation, up the Hudson, soon came to be known as Albany, instead of Orange—and what is more to the purpose, the tribe of Indians, spoken of, became known as the Minsies instead of the Minquas.

This is the name they were first known by in Eager's History of Orange County, and he says it signified: people living on a low tract of land, from which the water had been drained—alluding to the legendary belief that the valley along the Delaware, occupied by them, had once formed the bottom of a vast lake, from which the water finally escaped by breaking through the mountains, at a place now known as the Water-Gap, in the Delaware. This, most probably, was the original meaning and derivation of the word Minisink; for it is easy to trace the connection from the old Dutch name of the *Minquas*, to its English translation the *Minsies*, and finally to its later and last corruption of the Indian tongue, *Minisink*. It was known by this latter name as early as 1694, as we find from a journal kept by Captain Arent Schuyler, of a visit made by him to that region; and as this is the first visit of a white man to that section, recorded in authentic history, I have thought

proper to give it entire, word for word, as it was most
probably written and spelled by the valiant Captain
himself, and as it may be found on p. 98, Vol. IV. of
Documents relating to the History of New York. Gov.
Fletcher, at the time, lorded it over the province by
authority of the Crown of England, and this journey
appears to have been taken at his command, for the purpose of ascertaining whether or no the French, who then
occupied Canada, and were continually warring with
the English, had not sent emissaries among the Minisink
Indians to bribe them to unite with the Canadian Indians to wage a war of extermination against the New
Yorkers, which they would be most capable of doing
from among their impenetrable fastnesses in the Shawangunk Mountains.

JOURNAL OF CAPTAIN ARENT SCHUYLER'S VISIT TO THE
MINISINK COUNTRY.

May it please your Excell:

In persuance to y^r Excell: commands I have been
in the Minissinck Country of which I have kept the following journal: vizt

1694 ye 3^d of Feb: I departed from New Yorke for
East New Jersey and came that night att Bergentown
where I hired two men and a guide.

Y^e 4th Sunday Morning. I went from Bergen &
travilled about ten English miles beyond Haghkingsack
to an Indian place called Peckwes.

Y^e 5th Monday. From Peckwes North and be West
I went about thirty two miles, snowing and rainy
weather.

Y^e 6tth Tuesday. I continued my journey to Mag-
gaghkamieck [the Indian name of the river Neversink,
which falls into the Delaware a little south of Port

Jervis] and from thence to within half a day's journey
to the Menissinck.

Y[e] 7th Wendsday.   About eleaven a clock I arrived
att the Minissinck, and there I mett with two of their
Sachems and severall other Indians of whome I enquired
after some news, if the French or their Indians had sent
for them or been in y[e] Menissinck Country.   Upon
w[ch] they answered that noe French nor any of the
French Indians were nor had been in the Menissinck
Country nor there abouts and did promise y[t] if y[e] French
should happen to come or y[t] they heard of it that they
will forthwith send a mesinger and give y[r] Excellency
notice thereof.

Inquireing further after news they told me that six
days agoe three Christians and two Shanwans Indians
who went about fifteen months agoe with Arnout Vielle
into the Shanwans Country were passed by the Menissinck going for Albany to fetch powder for Arnout and
his company; and further told them that s[d] Arnout
intended to be there wth seaven hundred of y[e] said
Shanwans Indians loaden wth beavor and peltries att
y[e] time y[e] Indian corn is about one foot high (which
may be in the month of June.)   .

The Menissinck Sachems further s[d] that one of their
Sachems & other of their Indians were gone to fetch
beavor & peltries which they had hunted; and having
heard no news of them are afraid y[t] y[e] Sinneques have
killed them for y[e] lucar of the beavor or because y[e]
Menissinck Indians have not been with y[e] Sinneques as
usual to pay their Dutty, and therefore desier y[t] your
Excellency will be pleased to order y[t] the Sinneques
may be told, not to molest or hurt y[e] Menissincks they
be willing to continue in amity with them.

In the afternoon I departed from y[t] Menissincks; the

8th, 9th & 10th of Feb. I travilled and came att Bergen in ye morning and about noone arrived att New Yorke.

This is may it please your Excell. the humble reporte of your Excellency's most humble serv^t

ARENT SCHUYLER.

Scarce one hundred and seventy-two years have passed since the above journey was taken, and the comparison between then and now may be taken as a fair index to the rapid improvement that has everywhere been striding over the American Continent. Then the journey occupied eight days—four in going and four in returning—and was accomplished by untiring perseverance, amid the gloomy depths of an interminable forest, peopled only by the wild men of nature, and the panthers, bears, wolves, and other beasts that then prowled in its recesses ; the trackless path pointed out by an Indian guide, and its winding way followed over mountains and across valleys, one continual swamp and woodland, through the bitter cold and wet of a storm of rain and snow. Now, the same journey from New York to Port Jervis may be accomplished in the short space of about three hours and a half, by simply stepping in one of the elegant cars of the New York and Erie Railway, and sitting down in one of the velvet-cushioned seats—taking no note of the blinding snow or driving rain that may be falling out of doors, and with nothing to do but lean back on the cushions and enjoy the rocking motion as you glide along—glance out of the cozy little windows at the snug farm-houses and cultivated fields, as they flit before your vision—no guide—no nothing to think of, but to be ready with your pasteboard when the conductor thrusts his hand before your eyes and drives away your dreamy reveries with the oft repeated cry of—" Tickets !"

If it be indeed true that the shades of those gone before sometimes revisit earth, what emotions of surprise and pleasure must we conjecture to fill the bosom of that sturdy old backwoodsman, Arent Schuyler, if his spirit should come back from the confines of the invisible world and repeat his journey to Port Jervis—then a desolate swamp, now a flourishing village—by riding on the cars, in these days of luxury and speed. O, that he could speak to us, we would find our wildest imaginings to fall short of the tide of wonder and delight that would overflow his soul!

CHAPTER II.

The early settlement of this region is shrouded in mystery. The surrounding mountains appear to have served as barriers to the encroachment of the whites, and after they had effected a lodging to have prevented a knowledge of their early transactions from coming to the ears of the historians of those times, until almost a generation of the first Minisink pioneers had passed away. Lord Bellomont, Governor of New York in 1701, says, in a letter to the lords of trade, that the country west of the Highlands, at that time, was a dense wilderness, there being but one house in all that section—on Captain Evan's grant, which was along the Hudson. This was the first house built within the present limits of the eastern part of Orange County, and as such, it is but just to glance a moment at the history of the builder. It was built some years before Bellomont's notice of it, by Col. Patrick Magregorie, a Scotchman, who came to America with a band of followers in 1684. They landed in Maryland, but like the majority of the early emigrants, were continually roving around in quest of a better location. Magregorie was next located at Perth Amboy, New Jersey; but this was no better suited to his taste, and, in 1685, he petitioned for leave to take up land within the bounds of Billop's Point, on Staten Island.

At the instance, it is said, of Governor Dongan, he was persuaded to relinquish that design and remove to the Highlands. While here he devoted himself to the Indian trade, and became master of the Indian language. The following year, 1686, he was appointed Muster Master General of the Militia of the Province of New York, and was next sent in command of a party to trade at Michilmakinac, but was intercepted on the way by a party in the French interest, and carried a prisoner to Montreal. The next year he was liberated by orders from France, and returned to New York. The next year, 1688, he was employed by Sir Edmund Andros, and commanded a company that operated against the Indians east of Pemaquid. When the troubles broke out between the Government and the Leisler party, he was sent to New York city; where he was killed, during the attempt to reduce a fort held by the Leisler party, March, 1691. He was buried with public honors, and this appears to have been the most he ever received for his great public services, for we find the lands he laid claim to, along the Hudson, were subsequently granted to Capt. John Evans, who married his daughter Katherine. The patent was afterward vacated, and his heirs experienced a long series of difficulties in getting their claim adjusted. Their patent was finally settled in the town of Cornwall, Orange County. He had three sons, Hugh, John and Patrick, and two daughters, Katherine and Jane.

What was known of Orange County, at that time, embraced the present County of Rockland, and was bounded on the North by Ulster County, which extended along the western slope of the Shawangunk mountains to the Delaware, and included the present town of Deerpark, then a part of the town of Mamakating. Accord-

ing to Eager's History, Orange County was organized
by act of General Assembly in 1683.   In a list of officers,
dated April 20th, 1693, it is stated that the County contained not over twenty families, and was under the protection of New York city (p. 28, vol. iv. Doc. relating
to the Colonial History of New York).   It was named
after William, Prince of Orange, who was crowned King
of England, in 1689.   Like all the unoccupied territory
in those days, it was parceled out in immense tracts to
favorites of the different Governors of the Province;
and, as this was done by authority of Letters Patent
from the Crown, so these tracts were called Patents.
Thus it was we came to hear of the Wawayanda Patent,
which included 150,000 acres, and was conveyed March
5th, 1703, during the reign of Queen Anne, to John
Bridges, and twelve others, by the twelve Indian chiefs
Rapingonick, Wawastawaw, Moghopuck, Comelawaw,
Nanawitt, Ariwimack, Kumbout, Claus, Chouckhass,
Chingapaw, Oshasquemonus, and Quiliapaw,—and the
Minisink Patent made by the same Indian chiefs.   The
Governor's approval was doubtless first secured, and
then the Indians were induced to place their marks to
the documents, perhaps, by means of a little rum and
tobacco; at all events, for a mere trifle, and thus a
favored few became owners of thousands of acres of the
most fertile land in the world—to-day worth millions
upon millions of dollars.   In this connection it is well
enough to revert to the fact that, two hundred and forty
years ago, the whole of the territory now occupied by
the city of New York, was purchased of the Indians by
the Dutch for twenty-four dollars; as is stated in the
following letter, dated Nov. 5th, 1626 (vol. i. Doc. relating to the Colonial History of New York, p. 37):

" High and Mighty Lord:

"Yesterday arrived here the Ship of Arms, of Amsterdam, which sailed from New Netherland out of the River Mauritius (Hudson), on the 23d September. They report that our people are in good heart and live in peace there; the women have also borne some children there. They have purchased the Island Manhattes from the Indians for the value of 60 guilders ($24); 'tis 11,000 morgens in size. They had all their grain sowed by the middle of May, and reaped by the middle of August. They send thence samples of summer grain: such as wheat, rye, barley, oats, buckwheat, canary seed, beans and flax. The cargo of the aforesaid ship is: 7246 Beaver skins, 178½ Otter skins, 675 Otter skins, 48 Mink skins, 36 wild cat skins, 33 Minks, 34 Rat skins and a considerable Oak timber and Hickory. Herewith High and Mighty Lords, be commended to the mercy of the Almighty.

" To the High and Mighty Lords, my Lords the States General at the Hague.

" Signed Your High Mightiness' obedient,

" P. SCHAGAN.

" Amsterdam, Nov. 5, 1626."

Imagine, if possible, the present value of that same Island of Manhattan, with its population of hundreds of thousands and its untold movable wealth.

In 1698, by order of Governor Bellomont, a census of the several counties of New York was taken by the Sheriffs and Justices of the Peace, (p. 420, vol. iv., Doc. relating to the Colonial History of New York,) and Orange County was found to contain 29 men, 31 women, 140 children, and 19 negroes or slaves. The present

site of the village of Newburgh was included in a patent
of 2190 acres, granted to nine Palatines, or Germans, in
1719, viz.: George Lockstead, Michael Weigand, Her-
man Shoreman, Christian Hennicke, the widow Cockertal,
Burgher Mynders, Jacob Webber, Johannes Fisher, and
Andries Valch.   A settlement had been commenced
some time before, (about 1712,) by a young lady named
Sarah Wells, on the Wawayanda Patent, near the banks
of the Otterkill.   She was an orphan adopted by Christopher Denn, one of the patentees, who lived at that
time in New Jersey, opposite Staten Island.   It became
necessary, in order to fix the title to the patent, that
some settlement should be made upon it; and thus it
was, by aiding to secure the interest of Denn in the tract,
that she has been chronicled in history as the first white
person who commenced a settlement on the tract.   At
the request of her benefactor, she traveled in a boat
from New York to the neighborhood of New Windsor,
and from thence on foot to the Otterkill, to superintend
the erection of a wigwam, or house, with no companions
but a few friendly Indian guides.   To more enhance our
admiration of her fearless intrepidity, it is but proper to
state that she was but sixteen years of age at the time.
Think of that journey, ye timid votaries of luxury, who,
even in the midst of friends and neighbors, tremble at
the bare thought of venturing alone out of doors after
nightfall!   Think of the repose she sought at night
upon the ground, the glimmering stars sparkling through
the foliage of the great forest, the dismal howl of the
wolf echoing fearfully through the glades, and the hoot
of the lonely owl varying the concord of heart-chilling
sounds; and this, too, forty or fifty miles from the presence of a white person, with no protectors but her savage
friends.   She afterwards married William Bull, settled

on a tract of about one hundred acres, which was set off to her by Denn as a recompense for her services in making the settlement; and, after a long life of usefulness, died aged 102 years 15 days. Her descendants, a short time since, started the project of erecting a suitable monument over her remains, which lie buried in the family yard in Hamptonburgh. (Eager's History of Orange County, p. 454.).

The Ordinance for holding Courts of Sessions and Pleas in Orange County, was granted March 8th, 1702, at Fort Anne, by Edward Viscount Combury, William Smith, Peter Schuyler and Sa. Th. Boughton, Esqs., of Council, and ratified and signed by Queen Anne, April 5th, 1703. The first courts were held at Orangetown, in what is now Rockland county. The first Session in Goshen was held in 1727, (Ib. p. 17.)

But while the population of Orange county was thus rapidly increasing, and new villages springing up almost weekly within its limits, the history of the Minisink region appears to have been shrouded in darkness. The Shawangunk mountains formed a barrier which for a long time, kept from the outside world a view of the tide of civilization and improvement that was going on, and shut from the page of history much knowledge of the early settlers of that locality. Its mountain ranges afforded a shelter to the Indians long after the cultivated fields and happy homes of the white man had usurped the wilds of Eastern Orange. Among its glades and gorges, the smoke of their wigwams and the glimmer of their council fires, continued to rise in security and friendly intercouse with the early Minisink pioneers, years after the sun of their supremacy had set from Maine to the Carolinas. It was in this region, too, that some of their most barbarous atrocities were committed, before yielding up the possession of their mountain fastnesses.

In 1756, we are informed, that in the winter and spring large and small parties of western Indians made frequent incursions into its territory, destroying a vast amount of property, and taking many lives. At the commencement of this war (the old French and Indian war in 1755) it was reported to possess a population of about thirty families, and included a tract of about forty miles up and down the Delaware and Neversink rivers. Indeed, there are good reasons for dating the settlement of this region previous to the year 1664. In 1697 a Patent was granted to Arent Schuyler for lands described as follows:

" A certain tract of land in the Minisink country, in the province of New York, called by the native Indians Warensaghskennick, otherwise called Maghawaemus; also a certain parcel of meadow, or vly, called by the Indians Warensaghskennick, situate, lying and being upon a certain run, called by the Indians, and known by the name of Minisink, before a certain Island called Menayack, which is adjacent to or near to a certain tract of land called by the Indians Maghakeneck, containing the quantity of one thousand acres and no more."

This, as will be seen, gave the holder authority to locate on any unappropriated land in the valley, for it describes in such general terms as to puzzle almost any one to fix its limits. Another of these floating patents was granted the same year to Jacob Codebeck, Thomas Swartout, Anthony Swartout, Bernardus Swartout, Jan Tys, Peter Germar and David Jamison. This was located in what was called Peenpack. Many of the descendants of these patents are still living in that locality, Codebeck now being known as Cuddeback, and Germar as Gumaer. Some of the settlers on these patents were

Huguenots, or Frenchmen, who had voluntarily exiled themselves from France on account of their religious opinions being in conflict with the ruling powers. This is the origin of that name as applied to a small village a short distance north of Port Jervis at the present day. The following letter chronicles the second recorded visit of a white man to this territory; and as it is valuable on account of the knowledge it imparts in regard to this history, I have copied it entire from page 49 of Eager's History of Orange County:

(Copy of letters from Samuel Preston, Esq., dated Stockport, June 6th and 14th, 1828.)

MINISINK, MINEHOLES, &C.

"In 1787 the writer went on his first surveying tour into Northampton County; he was deputed under John Lukens, Surveyor General, and received from him, by way of instructions, the following narrative respecting the settlement of Minisink on the Delaware, above the Kittany and Blue Mountain: That the settlement was formed for a long time before it was known to the Government at Philadelphia. That when the Government was informed of the settlement, they passed a law in 1729, that any such purchases of the Indians should be null and void; and the purchasers indicted for forcible entry and detainer, according to the law of England. That in 1730 they appointed an agent to go and investigate the facts; that the agent so appointed was the famous surveyor, Nicholas Scull; that he, James Lukens, was Nicholas Scull's apprentice to carry chain and learn surveying. That as they both understood and could talk Indian they hired Indian guides, and had a fatiguing journey, there being then no white inhabitants in the upper part of Bucks or Northampton Counties. That
2

they had very great difficulty to lead their horses
through the water gap to Minisink flats, which were
all settled with Hollanders; with several they could
only be understood in Indian.   At the venerable
Depuis' they found great hospitality and plenty of the
necessaries of life.   J. Lukens said that the first thing
that struck his attention was a grove of apple trees of
size far beyond any near Philadelphia.   That as Nicholas
Scull and himself examined the banks, they were fully of
opinion that all those flats had at some former age been
a deep lake before the river broke through the mountain, and that the best interpretation they could make
of Minisink, was, *the water is gone.*   That S. Depuis told
them when the rivers were frozen he had a good road
to Esopus, near Kingston, from the Mineholes, on the
Mine road, some hundred miles.   That he took his wheat
and cider there for salt and necessaries, and did not appear to have any knowledge or idea where the river
ran (Philadelphia market) or of being in the government
of Pennsylvania.

"They were of opinion that the first settlements of
Hollanders in Minisink were many years older than
William Penn's charter, and that S. Depuis had treated
them so well, they concluded to make a survey of his
claim, in order to befriend him if necessary.   When
they began to survey, the Indians gathered around; an
old Indian laid his hand on Nicholas Scull's shoulder
and said: 'Put up iron string, go home.'   They then quit
and returned.

" I had it in charge from John Lukens to learn more
particulars respecting the Mine road to Esopus, &c.   I
found Nicholas Depuis, Esq., son of Samuel, living in a
spacious stone house in great plenty and affluence.
The old Mineholes were a few miles above, on the Jersey

side of the river by the lower point of Paaquarry Flat; that the Minisink settlement extended forty miles or more· on both sides of the river. That he had well known the Mine road to Esopus, and used, before he opened the boat channel through Foul Rift, to drive on it several times every winter with loads of wheat and cider, as also did his neighbors, to purchase his salt and necessaries, in Esopus, having then no other market or knowledge where the river ran to. That after a navigable channel was opened through Foul Rift they generally took to boating, and most of the settlement turned their trade down stream, the Mine road became less and less traveled.

"This interview with the amiable Nicholas Depuis, was in June, 1787. He then appeared about sixty years of age. I interrogated as to the particulars of what he knew, as to when and by whom the Mine road was made, what was the ore they dug and hauled on it, what was the date, and from whence or how, came the first settlers of Minisink in such great numbers as to take up all the flats on both sides of the river for forty miles. He could only give traditionary accounts of what he had heard from older people, without date, in substance as follows:

" That in some former age there came a company of miners from Holland; supposed, from the great labor expended in making that road, about one hundred miles, that they were very rich or great people, in working the two mines—one on the Delaware, where the mountain nearly approaches the lower point of Paaquarry Flat—the other at the north foot of the same mountain, near half way from the Delaware and Esopus. He ever understood that abundance of ore had been hauled on that road, but never could learn whether lead or silver,

That the first settlers came from Holland to seek a place
of quiet, being persecuted for their religion.   I believe
they were Armenians.   They followed the Mine road to
the large flats on the Delaware.   That smooth, cleared
land suited their views.   That they *bona fide* bought
the improvements of the native Indians, most of whom
then moved to the Susquehanna; that with such as
remained, there was peace till 1755.   I then went to
view the Paaquarry Mineholes.   There appeared to have
been a great abundance of labor done there at some
former time, but the mouths of these holes were caved
full, and overgrown with bushes.   I concluded to myself
if there ever was a rich mine under that mountain, it
must be there yet, in close confinement.   The other old
men I conversed with, gave their traditions similar to
Nicholas Depuis, and they all appeared to be grandsons
of the first settlers, and very ignorant as to the dates,
and things relating to chronology.   In the summer of
1789 I began to build on this place; then came two venerable gentlemen on a surveying expedition.   They
were the late Gen. James Clinton, the father of the late
DeWitt Clinton, and Christopher Tappan, Esq., Clerk
and Recorder of Ulster County.   For many years before
they had both been surveyors under Gen. Clinton's
father, when he was Surveyor-General.   In order to
learn some history from gentlemen of their general
knowledge, I accompanied them in the woods.   They
both well knew the Mineholes, Mine road, &c., and as
there were no kind of documents or records thereof,
united in the opinion that it was a work transacted
while the State of New York belonged to the government of Holland; that it fell to the English in 1664;
and that the change of government stopped the mining
business, and that the road must have been made many

years before such digging could have been done. That it undoubtedly must have been the first good road of that extent made in any part of the United States."

The settlement principally spoken of by the above writer, was on the Pennsylvania side of the Delaware river, and visited from Philadelphia; but applies to the whole Minisink region. It discloses to our view a perfect miniature world—peopled by a happy, contented race of Europeans ; who for generations had lived in harmony among themselves, and in peace with their savage neighbors. Here generations lived the fleeting span of life in blissful ignorance of any outer or happier world beside, and were alike unknown outside the boundaries of their own domain, until some wanderer chanced to come across their settlement, and went on his way, thereafter to remember, with gratitude and envy, the affluence and comfort that marked their rough but happy homes. No fashions from abroad intruded upon their attire, or simple hospitality—their customs were their own—their visits made among familiar friends— their parties and soirees given in true Minisink state, and no doubt better enjoyed by the homespun-clad young folks of that time, than many a skim-milk gathering of the present day. Here they were born and reared, from infancy to mature years: married the partners of their choice;

" Lived where their fathers lived,
And died where they died:
Lived happy—died happy,"

and perhaps have gone to a happy home above.

Plenty of mineral resources were within their reach, but they seem to have wisely left such pursuits to later and more speculative times. Whether those early mines produced lead or silver, is not known: but we are

of opinion that it may have been silver, for the following
reasons: First, the great length of road (one hundred
miles) would have rendered next to impossible the cart-
ing of such a bulky substance as lead, in any great quantity, or at least in sufficient quantities to have paid
expenses—let alone liquidating the cost of constructing
such a road as this was represented to be, and in places
still is, through a wilderness. Second, all the old traditions of those times confirm the belief that silver ore
exists in Shawangunk Mountain, and that at early
periods, mines of it were known and worked by the
Indians and first settlers, that have since been concealed
and forgotten. We once heard an old gentleman describe
one of these mines that must have been located near
one of those spoken of by the writer of the preceding
letter. It was made known to his father, and a neighbor, by one of the friendly Indians previous to their
removal west in the old Indian war. The two observed
great secrecy in working it, and frequently made long
and mysterious journeys to dispose of their ore at distant places. At last the Revolutionary war broke out,
and they both determined to serve their country. Before departing, they solemnly pledged themselves not
to reveal the secret until the war was ended; and the
better to carry out their plans, they went, one cold, dark
night, and drew a large flat stone over the mouth of the
mine, carefully obliterated all traces of their work, and
ended by strewing leaves over the whole, until they
themselves could hardly detect its whereabouts. About
thirty paces directly east, they marked three trees that
stood close together, in order to guide them, should
either live to again desire to find it. One of them never
returned; the other again sought his home after an
absence of near nine years. Meanwhile the tide of

war had visited his old neighborhood in the shape of predatory bands of Indians, and he found his family in a distant village where they had fled for protection— his house, and that of his neighbors, having been destroyed by their foes. A year or so was occupied in again getting around them the comforts of a home, and when he again sought the mine, the timber had been so destroyed by the fire and ruthless vandalism, that no trace of the marked trees could be found. Days and weeks were spent in the search, but in vain. He then gave the information to others, but no one has ever yet removed the flat stone from the mouth of the silver mine.

Another old gentleman, while we were staying in Wurtsboro' one evening, gave us a somewhat flowery account of a silver mine, which we will notice. The settlers in that vicinity had long noticed that the Indians had plenty of silver in a crude state, but could get no trace of the mine. Just before they left the country, our narrator's father, then a youth of twelve or thirteen years of age, persuaded an old Indian chief, with whom he was a great favorite, to take him to it. He was blindfolded, and led a long way through the woods, with many twists and turns, till at last they commenced going down into the heart of the mountain, and he could distinctly hear water trickling overhead. When his eyes were uncovered he stood before a solid vein of silver. Picking up a number of large pieces, his conductor forced him to return in the same manner as he entered; and though afterwards he searched for it, over every foot of ground near its supposed vicinity, he could never find it. "Every seven years," quoth our friend, "a bright light, like a candle, rises at twelve o'clock at night, above the mine, and disappears in the clouds.

But no one that has seen it, has ever been able, in daylight, to find from whence it rose."

CHAPTER III.

Like all the rest of the human family, the inhabitants of Minisink naturally felt a little anxious as to where their final lot would be cast in the world of spirits; for tradition had handed down to them the lessons of their forefathers in their own fatherland, and many an old bible and hymn book that had, perhaps, spoken sharply to the consciences of their ancestors on the banks of the Zuyder Zee, in Holland, or by the side of the Seine, in sunny France—done duty through long nights of fearful peril on the bosom of the stormy Atlantic, and consoled the minds of sinners miserably sea-sick during the first weeks of the months that then were required to place them from the old continent on the new—even yet spoke in trumpet-tones to the evil-doers by the banks of the Delaware and Neversink. Though the leaves were perhaps worn and soiled, and it may be somewhat torn, the old bible still spoke to them in a voice that was as stern and as strong as when of yore it reproved the sins of their grandfathers and grandmothers. It pointed just as unerringly to the lake prepared of fire and brimstone for those that turned aside from the path of rectitude. Its warnings were not to be disregarded—for

2*

though apparently a community outside the pale of the
civilized world, they knew that the eye of Divine Providence was just as watchful of the affairs of the few
settlers on the Minisink flats, as of those of Amsterdam
or Paris.   At first neighbors talked of it when they met,
and their good dames discussed it of evenings while
enjoying a sociable visit.   Then it became talked of
generally; and finally a meeting of the veteran settlers
was called, and it was determined to have preaching
and psalm-singing, such as their fathers and mothers told
them they had often listened to of a Sabbath, 'neath the
roof of a church in their own native land.   Every one
contributed to the good work,—the old men and women
because they felt it their duty,—the young men and
women because they liked some place to repair to on
the Sabbath, where they could unite their voices in
hymns of praise, and perchance find opportunities of
speaking a word or two with each other on the sly; for
the young people of that day probably possessed the
same feelings as those of to-day, though far less burdened
with fashionable hypocrisy.   It was agreed that the
community was large enough for four congregations, and
accordingly it was so divided.   The means was collected,
and the construction of the four churches was probably
commenced in 1736.   A young man among them, John
Casparus Fryenmuth, who had been studying with the
intention of becoming a minister, was furnished with
funds to go to Holland, where he completed his studies
and was ordained.   He returned and became pastor of
the four congregations in the year 1742.   The first
church was called the Mackhackemeck Church; and was
located about a half mile south of where Port Jervis
now stands, and about half a mile from the junction of
the Neversink and Delaware, in a north-easterly direc-

tion, and near the residence of Mr. Eli Van Inwegen, by the old burying-ground. The second stood about eight miles south-west from the Mackhackemeck, in the present township of Montague, or Sandiston, N. J., at the crossing of the turnpike and highway, near the site of a store kept for some years by one Judge Stull, and was called the Minisink Church. It was torn down many years ago, and a new one erected about one mile from its first location, due north. The third stood sixteen miles farther on in New Jersey, and was called the Walpeck Church. It has long been torn down. The fourth was eight or ten miles distant from the Walpeck, and was called the Smithfield Church. Before having a regular minister, at their meetings the best reader was selected, and a chapter or two read from the Bible, a prayer or so was made by different members, and some psalm-singing commonly completed the services. The hour of worship was announced by the blowing of a large tin horn, kept for the purpose, which practice was adhered to until bells came in use.

Mackhackemeck Church was the only one of the four that stood within the present limits of Orange county; and as such, its history is important, being probably the oldest.. It is of the Dutch Reformed persuasion, that being the almost universal belief at the time of its erection. This event was brought to a completion in 1737 judging from the fact that it was formally recognized, and had regular ecclesiastical officers in that year, as shown by the records of baptisms, &c., that are still in good preservation. These records were kept in the Low Dutch language until recently, and are continuous from that year to the present. The building of the church took place near a century from the date of the supposed first settlement of the Minisink region. John

Casparus Fryenmuth, the first minister, officiated for the four churches mentioned (as his successors did also for many years,) from 1742, the date of his return from Holland, till 1755; when the French and Indian war commenced, and predatory bands began to plunder and devastate the settlement, which rendered it unsafe to continue the services. He was a good scholar, and a beautiful penman; the records kept by him being splendid specimens of writing, and his name, as signed to them by himself, one hundred and twenty-four years ago, can still be seen, in a bold round hand that few persons can equal at the present day, with all the improvement of knowledge and science. The first capital letter of his signature was always made in the form of a monogram (a figure combining in one the initials of the name). He was very much respected and popular, if we may believe the traditions of the times. Of the esteem felt for him by his parishioners, one incident has been handed down to us, and we believe it is the only one preserved of his ministry. He had been in the habit of dividing the time of his vacation, a short period of a few Sabbaths allowed the minister yearly for rest, (as we understand from Rev. S. W. Mills, the present pastor, to whom our thanks are due for many of these particulars,) among the churches in the vicinity of Rochester, Ulster county. They became desirous of securing his services for themselves, and accordingly set themselves about raising a salary for him by subscription, previous to giving him a call. This the Minisink people heard of, and the way they talked to the Rochester people, is best shown in the following letter preserved among the church records in the original Dutch, of which this is a translated copy:

"Minisink, Dec. 6th, 1741.

" *To the Rev. Consistory of Rochester, greeting:*

" We, your servants, having learned that you have had correspondence with our pastor, and have seduced him, so far as to send him a call, thinking that the large amount of salary promised him will induce him to leave us—the Lord who thus far has caused your acts of supplanting to fail will further direct them to a good end. We find ourselves bound to obey the command of the Saviour ' Do good to them that hate you ;' we therefore will deal with you hereafter, as we have before, 'doing you good.' It is true you give us no thanks for his services among you. You are bold enough to say that he has eight free Sundays during the year, which is as true as the assertion of the Devil to Eve, 'You will not surely die.'

" If you desire, then, to have our minister four or six times during the year, we will grant your wish cheerfully, and leave it with our pastor to settle with you as to the amount of his compensation. If this cannot prevent the execution of your unjust intention, and the Lord wishes to use you as a rod to chasten us, we shall console ourselves with his gracious words, Heb. 12. 'Whom the Lord loveth he chasteneth, and he rebukes every son whom he adopts.' If it please the Lord to permit you to deprive us of our pastor, then we hope that your consciences will not be seared so much as to take away our livelihood amounting to £125 12s. 6d. (over paid salary).

" Should this however be the case, then we will not hesitate to give the matter into the hands of a worldly judge. We expect your answer, and conclude our discourse with the wish that the grace of our Lord and

the love of God the Father, and the communion of the
Holy Ghost, may remain with you until a blessed
eternity. Amen. We remain your servants,

> " JOHN CORTRIGHT,
> " JOHN VAN VLIET,
> " ABM. VAN RAMPEN,
> " WILLIAM COLE."

Whether this unique letter settled the matter or not,
is not known ; but Mr. Fryenmuth remained with the
Minisinkers.   After leaving Minisink, his whereabouts is
involved in mystery; though he probably visited that
section afterward, as his handwriting appears in the
records at later dates.   Lastly, August 26th, 1759, when
he probably made his last visit.

After the Indian troubles had partially subsided and
a state of comparative quiet had been restored, Rev.
Thomas Romeyn was selected to minister to the spiritual
wants of the people of Minisink.   He accepted the call
September 6th, 1760, (as we learn from a letter of one of
his descendants,) and was officiating minister until 1772,
a period of twelve years, when he removed to Cahnawaga,
Montgomery County, N. Y.   The five years intervening
between Mr. Fryenmuth's departure and Mr. Romeyn's
arrival, appears to have been almost a blank in church
affairs.

During Mr. Romeyn's charge, these affairs, that till
then had glided along so smoothly and uninterruptedly,
partook of the spirit from abroad, and followed the
course generally ascribed to the carnal world, and in
weak imitation of poor sinful human nature, became
embroiled in a quarel of surprising bitterness.

The Dutch Reformed Church in this country had
hitherto been subordinate to the classes of Amsterdam,
in Holland; and all ministers desirous of being ordained,

had to proceed there for that purpose. A large portion
of the members were in favor of continuing that practice,
and were called the Conferentic party. The others
were in favor of ordaining their ministers by classes in
this country, thus saving the expense and formality of a
trip to Europe. These went under the cognomen of
the Coetus party. The first meeting of ministers to
settle the question was held in the City of New York
in the year 1737. Another was held the following year
which decided in favor of the Coetus party, and sent their
decision to the classes of Amsterdam for approval. The
latter was finally confirmed in 1746, and thus the wing
of the church in this country became independent of
that of Holland.

The first Coetus, or classes, for the ordination of ministers and other business, was held in September, 1747.
Under this new order all ministers were to be re-ordained,
and a general overhauling of church affairs took place.
The Conferentic party in Minisink were determined to
hold the ascendency, and the Coetus party as fully
determined they should not. The Coetus party insisted
that in obedience to the new order all children should
be rebaptized, and this developed a new feature in the
ferment and added to its bitterness. The ladies of the
Conferentic party declared they would not submit to
this—it was bad enough to insult their ministers by
forcing them to be re-ordained—but to cause the very
babes to be re-baptized was an unheard of barbarity.
Nobly did they maintain their ground.

A young man, of the Coetus party, was waiting upon
a young lady of good family, who, with her parents, was
strongly attached to the opposite party. The match
progressed favorably. The young lady returned his
affection, and gave her consent to an early marriage.

Her parents did not object, and everything bid fair for a prosperous voyage upon the sea of life. But, alas! how easy it is for disappointment to intervene. One Sunday evening, as usual, the young man was wending his way to the residence of his betrothed. But about two weeks more were between him and the consummation of his cherished hopes. He determined on this evening to settle all little preliminaries, so that no misunderstanding might occur on some more important occasion. His intended met him at the door with her brightest smile of welcome, and ere long both found themselves alone in the best room before the sparkling fire.

" And so, dearest Jane," said he, putting an arm around her neck, and snatching a kiss from her tempting lips, " so two weeks must pass by before I can call you my bonny wife. How long the time will seem."

" No, John," said she, " it will pass quick enough, for it may be, after we are married, you will not always think the same of me that you do now."

" Ah, you little rogue, how can I ever think less of you ? But, by the way, my darling, I thought I would speak to you about the dominie we are to have to marry us. I think we had better get Mr. ——" (naming a minister of the Coetus party.)

" And I have been thinking that Mr. Romeyn was the one we ought to get. He's a neighbor of ours, and preaches here in Maghackameck Church."

" But I don't like him," said John.

" We think he is a good man," said Jane.

" But he is a Conferentie," persisted John.

" And so am I a Conferentie," returned Jane indig-nantly, as she drew herself from his embrace.

" But I won't have him," remarked John, rashly, as he began to feel his ireful nature rise,

" Then you won't have me," was Jane's rejoinder.

" I can get along without you, I'll let you understand," said John, independently, as he began to look for his hat, and to move toward the door.

" You're a good for nothing scamp, so you are," sobbed Jane, snappishly.

"I am glad I have found you out before it was too late," quoth John, as he made his exit from the door. " I am glad of it——"

" And so am I glad of it," said Jane, determinedly; and she shut the door behind him and cut in twain his half finished sentence.

This true incident of the ill feeling engendered by the controversy, did not terminate as all lover's quarrels generally do—in reconciliation—for tradition has it that they held good the grudge to the day of their death. Nor was the ill feeling among the members, productive of such notable results in this vicinity alone. It is recorded that an equally amusing incident took place at Hackensack, New Jersey, though of a different nature.

Mr. Goetschius, the minister at that place, took sides with the Conferentics, and announced himself an advocate of their measures. Hereat a great commotion arose, and the "pillars" of the church in the interest of the Coetus party, headed by the clerk, immediately assumed a pugilistic position. The preaching they had listened to, for hours at a time, with respectful attention and composure, they now declared to have been a decided bore. The opinions they had endorsed, and the sayings they had so often quoted as the productions of a genius possessed alone by their beloved dominie, they now discovered to have been sheer nonsense, and the author a numbscull. The common reply to a question often asked at gatherings, as to how the dominie was liked,

had been : " O, he is a very smart man; I don't see how
any one can help liking him;" now assumed the form of
an every-day remark, " How dull the minister is, lately:
I can't bear to listen to his preaching."

In short, the minister who had before been classed
among the race of humans known as " smart men," was
now stoutly asserted to " know no more than he ought
to," by the very ones who, a short time before, had been
his warmest supporters. So much does a difference of
opinion change the hearts of men. To counterbalance
this tide of criticism, the dominie launched from the
pulpit his sharpest thrusts at the doctrines of his antag-
onists. His opponents retaliated by staying at home
and ridiculing the smallness of his congregation. The
dominie waxed warm in the cause as his hearers grew
small in numbers, and hurled logic in chunks of the
largest dimensions in the teeth of his foes. They found
themselves necessitated to do something to prevent
being outwinded by his reverence, and had recourse to
a strategy often effectual when milder means fail—
namely, they resolved to choke him off. The clerk held
the keys of the church—nothing was easier—so the next
time the minister came to fulfill an appointment, he
found the doors loocked. On one or two occasions after
this he succeeded in gaining admittance, and held forth
triumphantly to the few persons comprising his audi-
ence. To remedy this his opponents provided themselves with a novel expedient. The next time he
succeeded in gaining admittance they were on hand in
full force, and the imperturbable clerk rose. as usual, to
give out the opening hymn. This he did by giving to
the singers the 119th psalm, which, in the mode of singing then in vogue, would have consumed the entire day.
This was something the dominie had not counted upon;

and, as a natural consequence, for some time it operated much as a knock-down blow is supposed to do in pugilistic parlance; but at length thinking enough singing had been done for one day, he rose—persisted in his efforts to be heard—overpowered the voices of the singers—succeeded in restoring silence, and again came off victorious. But, after all, his triumphs were productive of such barren results that he was at last forced to succumb, and in the end the clerk and his friends carried the day.

Other instances were known where opposing partisans met with their teams in the road and refused to turn out, till one or the other became tired of waiting and had to yield the right of way, vowing all sorts of future revenge.

Nor did the disturbance fail to reach the position of Mr. Romeyn. Being a member of the Conferentie party, his opponents assailed him much in the manner of the Hackensack dominie, but not in such violent terms. They listened to his preaching and respected his talents, but succeeded in getting him removed in the year 1771.

By this time the excitement had run its length, and in the following year almost wholly subsided, after having been a potent spirit of dissension for more than thirty years.

Mr. Thomas Romeyn was born at Pumpton, N. J., March 20, 1729. He commenced his studies for the ministry April, 1747. He sailed from New York to Europe April 11th, 1752; and was ordained by the Classis at Amsterdam, Sept. 3, of the same year. He must have immediately sailed for America, for he accepted a call Nov. 10, of the same year, at Flatbush, Long Island. June 29, 1756, he was married to Margaret

Frelinghuyson, daughter of the Rev. Theodore Frelinghuyson. His eldest son, Theodore, was born Nov. 28,
1757; and his mother died the 25th day of the following
month.

Mr. Romeyn came to Minisink Sept. 6th, 1760, and
married his second wife, Susannah Van Compton, daughter of Col. Abm. Van Compton, of Paquary, Oct. 30, of
the same year. By his last wife he had six sons—Abraham, born Aug. 9, 1761, about three miles below the
brick house, New Jersey, Nicholas, James V. C., John,
Benjamin and Thomas. He went to Cahnawaga, N. Y.,
in 1772, where he officiated as minister for one year;
when he was disabled by the palsy, we believe, and died
October 22, 1794.

Three of his sons entered the ministry. Theodore
settled at Somerville, New Jersey, where he died at the
age of 29. James was pastor of the church at Hackensack, New Jersey, thirty-three years, and died June,
1840. The sixth son studied for the ministry, but died
at the age of twenty-two. The seventh son was pastor
of the church at Niskawgna, a little north of Albany, and
was living June 9, 1855, aged seventy-eight years. For
thirteen or fourteen years after his leaving Minisink, a
blank occurs.

Rev. Elias Van Benschoten was installed as pastor of
Mackhackemeck church August 28, 1785. The church
had been burned by Brandt's Indians in 1779, and the
second church was built during the first two years of
Van Benschoten's pastorate, near the site of the first.
In 1793 an inventory of the church property was made,
as follows:

                               " *March* 29, 1793.

" An inventory of all the estate, both real and personal, with the annual revenue arising thereon, belonging

to the Dutch Reformed Church of Mackhackemeck, in the County of Orange:

"One acre of ground, with the church on it, without any annual revenue from the seats.

"Third part of 23 acres and some parts of an acre of ground, with a house and barn on it, which the minister possesses for the time being as part of his salary.

"Between £44 and £45 subscribed yearly to pay to the elders and deacons of said church, and by them to be paid unto our present minister while he resides among us.

"One Bible, one Psalm book, one book of records.

"Sabbath day collection in bank £2 15s. 9d.

"One little trunk.

(Here follows a certificate stating the inventory to have been exhibited to William Wickham, one of the judges of the Court of Common Pleas for Orange county.)

"Sworn to March }
    29th, 1793.   }
"William Wickham."

"Benjamin Depuy,
"Harmanus Van Inwegen,
"Johannes Decker,
"Wilhelmus Cole,
"Martinus Decker."

The little trunk mentioned is in good preservation. and its countenance as unruffled as though but two years, instead of seventy-three, had passed over it.

Mr. Van Benschoten's pastoral relations were dissolved, we believe, in 1795; though he probably remained in the vicinity till after 1800. He died near Deckertown, N. J., where he owned a farm.

Rev. John Demarest was his successor in 1803–4, and remained till about 1808.

Rev. Cornelius C. Elting, the fifth in order, came to Mackhackemeck January 25, 1817, aged twenty-four years, and continued the services till he died, October

24th, 1843. During his stay, in 1834, the present edifice was built—the land being donated by the Delaware and Hudson Canal Company. In 1838 the name was changed by act of the legislature to the "Dutch Reformed Church of Deerpark."

Rev. George P. Van Wyck became his successor February 29, 1844. He remained till 1852. Rev. Hiram Slawson succeeded him February 22, 1853. Rev. S. W. Mills is the present incumbent, a notice of whose family will be found in chapter xi. of this work.

The inhabitants of the Minisink region have become sadly diverse in religious matters since the building of the old church one hundred and twenty-nine years ago; and instead of four churches, numbers of them now abound of different denominations. But though they now have more modern appliances for worship,—costlier buildings of more fashionable exterior—huge bells of sounding brass—seats cushioned and pulpits trimmed with softest velvet, and organs tuned to greatest harmony,—how much more sincere seems the rude piety of our Minisink ancestry, whose four churches were built for convenience without regard to fashion—the seats in them being undoubtedly of rough boards; whose only music was the voices of fathers, mothers, sisters and brothers, sending anthems of praise in Nature's melody up to Nature's God; and the hour of worship announced on a Sabbath morning by the far echoing notes of a simple *tin horn!*

> " No sculptured marble marked the place
>   Where God's high altar stood;
>   It rose with unassuming grace
>   Of plain unpainted wood."

CHAPTER IV.

The heroic people of this region did not suffer their minor difficulties to hinder them from defending their rights against all foes, whether native or foreign; and for a period of sixty-seven years, fought a war second to none in the brilliancy of the strategical operations, and daring achievements—though the number of the slain may not have equaled the number of the one battle of the Wilderness, or their generals the fame of a Sherman or a Grant. The war partook of the general character of a border fray, and arose from a dispute in regard to the boundary line between New York and New Jersey.

Charles II., King of England, gave his brother, the Duke of York, afterward King James II., a patent of all the lands " from the West side of the Connecticut River to the East side of Delaware Bay," dated March 12th, 1663. On June 24th of the following year, the Duke granted by lease and release all the tract of country now known as New Jersey—then called *Nova Cæsarea* (so described in the patent)—to John, Lord Berkley, and Sir George Cartaret, bounded as follows: " Southward to the main ocean as far as Cape May at the mouth of the Delaware, then along said River or Bay to the Northward as far as the Northwardmost branch of the said Bay or River, which is in latitude 41 deg. 40 min., and crosseth over thence in a straight line to the latitude 41 deg., on Hudson's River."

Cartaret took the east half of the province and Berkley the west, and thus it became called East and West New Jersey. The Dutch re-conquered New York in 1673, and this territory again came into their possession; but a treaty of peace being concluded February 9, 1674, between England and Holland, it was restored to the English. Sir George Cartaret immediately took the precaution of having a new patent made out the 29th of July following the treaty of peace, and the boundaries were again defined in about the same general terms as before.

A discussion soon arose as to which should be considered the "Northwardmost branch" of the Delaware river. All agreed on a point on the Hudson river, in latitude 41 deg.; but the New York men insisted that the line should reach the Delaware at the southern extremity of what is called Big Minisink Island, and the Jerseymen as stoutly contended that it should touch the Delaware a little south of where Cochecton now stands—thus leaving a territory in dispute several miles wide at the west end, and tapering to a point at the east. This included a good part of the Minisink region. The proprietors, under the New Jersey government, parceled out the land in tracts to different persons, and these came on to assume possession. The Minisink people having enjoyed possession for a long time refused to agree to this, and determined to maintain their claims. Recrimination and retaliation followed, and a general border warfare took place. Numbers of the Minisink people were taken prisoners and lodged in the prisons of New Jersey, and a state of alarm and danger prevailed.

The men went constantly armed, prepared to defend themselves to the last extremity, and keeping a constant lookout for the appearance of their meddlesome foes.

The first regular series of engagements of much notoriety that is recorded, resulted from the efforts made to obtain possession of the lands of one Major Swartout, between the years 1730 and 1740. The Major was a true gentleman of the old school, a hale, bluff old pioneer. He was major of the militia of Orange county, and when parade days came around, none presented a more military appearance. The people of Goshen, where the military parades then took place, as fully considered the major a part of the occasion as they were certain that the day came round. It was then he was in his element. Mounted on his powerful horse, at the head of his men, his doughty limbs and portly frame encased in military toggery resplendent in brass buttons, a sword of monstrous length dangling from his waist and flapping against his horse's side with every jolt, his head encased in a huge cocked hat, over which a feather flaunted proudly, and from under which his eyes twinkled with the importance of his position, the Major justly carried the palm of superiority in his profession, and presented a model which but few officers, with all modern inventions, have been able to copy successfully even at the present day. His lands were in the disputed territory, and threats were made time and again by the Jerseymen that they meant to drive the Major off. He however took the matter coolly, slept soundly through the wars and rumors of wars that reached his ears, and assured his friends at Goshen that he was not afraid, in reply to a prophesy that he would come into Goshen some morning homeless. His neigh-

3

bors stood ready to lend their help whenever called on, and the knowing ones shook their heads and hinted that the "Jersey Blues" would have a lively time in getting hold of the Major's land. But the enemy were crafty, and one day when the neighbors were absent on some public occasion, made a charge on the Major's fortress, and before he could form his family in line of battle, much less draw his "trusty blade," he found himself, his family and household goods, residents of an exceeding large residence—the timbers thereof not made with hands, the roof the blue heavens, and the rooms large and airy to a fault—in fact found himself out of doors. A pretty predicament this, for the major of the Orange county militia. Besides, the Major had made quite extensive preparations for this very attack; having kept a number of loaded muskets ready for use, and several extra hired men on the farm to defend it; and to be thus outgeneraled reflected somewhat on his military prowess. But he was not the man to despond; so removing his family to a neighbor's house he set off for help, and one fine morning the people of Goshen were surprised to see the redoubtable Major come riding down the street looking greatly chopfallen, and altogether devoid of that erect, martial air, so much the admiration of his men.

The intelligence of his disaster sped with lightning rapidity, and in a short time a formidable company had volunteered to reinstate him in his own house. Arriving in the vicinity it was judged best to employ a little strategy, and the whole company crept as close as possible to the house without being discovered. They then sent Peter Gumaer to the house as a sort of reconnoitering party, to see if everything was favorable. If so, he was to come out of the house, and while going through the orchard throw up an apple, as a signal for the attack. Mr. Gumaer was gone some time, every moment of which was passed in anxious expectation by the heroes of the ambush. At last they saw him come out of the house, and as he passed through the orchard, give the required signal. Simultaneously they made a rush, with a yell of defiance that would have done credit to a band of Minisink Indians. The occupants of the house were totally unprepared; even had it been otherwise it would have availed them nothing. Right on came the Major, puffing and blowing with the extraordinary exercise of a double-quick, and the effort needed to keep an upright position, owing to the scabbard of his big sword so frequently getting entangled with his legs—while behind him came his company, in an irregular line, but with a determination visible to do or to die. Right on they came with an impetuosity that stopped at no impediment! On they came over the beet and onion beds in the garden; over the door-yard fence, and the flower beds in the door yard !—on !—on they charged right up to the very door. The fastenings gave way before the pressure, and in less time than it takes to tell it, the inmates were taken by the napes of their necks and walked out-doors—the Major claiming the privilege of bestowing three or four hearty kicks upon the ringleader's rear, as a parting admonition when he stepped from the door. Their goods were quickly thrown out after them, and thus was this decisive victory gained without the loss of a single man.

Knowing that this would be followed by a more extensive raid, the people of Minisink procured the services of a spy, who lived among the Jersey claimants, some twenty miles distant, and thus got information of their intended movements in time to frustrate them.

The Major's son-in-law, one Harmanus Van Inwegen, also acquired considerable fame during this struggle. He is recorded to have been a very bold, intrepid man, and to have possessed great strength. As an instance of this it is stated that on one occasion, while at work in the field, word was brought to him that some Indians were at his house abusing his family. He at once repaired to the house, and entering it abruptly, grappled with the Indians, and after a sharp hand-to-hand struggle, succeeded in overpowering and driving them from the house by main strength alone. This was the more courageous from the fact that the Indians were armed with guns and attempted to shoot him frequently during the contest.

About 1740, word was conveyed to the Minisink people that the "Jersey Blues" contemplated a grand raid on the disputed territory during the fall of that year, and preparations were made to give them a warm reception. On the day of the expected attack, the owners of the territory, with their sons and relatives, collected at the house of Harmanus Van Inwegen. They were well armed and equipped, and met seriously with the determination of maintaining their rights. Major Swartout was unanimously chosen commander, and proceeded to organize the forces. They were deployed in double column fronting the direction of the expected attack, the right and left wings under command of Jacob Cuddeback and old Mr. Van Inwegen, respectively. They were both as resolute as the Major, and when their positions were assigned them, took their places in front of the line; remarking, that as they were old men their lives were not so valuable as those of the young, and they desired to occupy the most exposed situations. **The Major then took his station in front, to lead and give**

the word of command. Never had he felt so proudly as
when on that eventful day he cast his eye along the well-
formed lines of his little army. Even the feather in his
cocked hat seemed to be aware of the important position it occupied, and danced lightly in the breeze as if
eager for the conflict. Especially did his eye rest with
delight on his wing commanders—they were his depend-
ence; for full well he understood, that the quickest way
to make an army fly is to break its wings; and these he
had reason to know would be the weakest parts of the
enemy's lines. Not long had they to wait. The enemy
soon made his appearance in strong force on the road.
His lines were well filled and the men looked stout and
well armed. Their commander too was a constable
from the land of Jersey—a man powerful in his own
estimation, and more especially so when armed as he
now was with the terrible majesty of authority conferred
by reason of the law. The Major, who had before felt
confident of an easy victory, now began to feel some
misgivings as to the result. The pommel of his sword,
upon which his hand rested, felt only about half as large
as before, and the feather in his cocked hat began to
smooth itself down behind the crown. On came the
constable and the Jerseymen in fearful array, though
somewhat dismayed at the unexpected force opposed to
them. The constable's nether lip began to lengthen
dubiously, and his knees to tremble in spite of himself;
but there was no backing out now. The distance began to
shorten visibly between the contending forces. Timid
ones began to cast anxious glances behind them and to
wish themselves anywhere but at that particular place.
Visions of past misdeeds floated through their minds,
coupled with the thought that a repentance would avail
nothing when brought about by fear alone. The dis-

tance lessened. A few moments more and the battle would begin. The forces are within gunshot. But see, the courage of the constable's men begins to waver— their steps grow shorter, and he commands a halt ! It was a moment of dread suspense. One word and death would most probably have visited the ranks of both parties. Gerardus Swartout, a son of the Major, not knowing whether it would be best to kill any of the foe, at this juncture called to his father to know how he should fire. The Major remembered their raid upon his house, and the death of his wife, who was sick at the time and who died afterwards from the effect of their hasty removal, and replied determinedly, "Kill them !" This was the finishing stroke; the Jerseymen had sup- posed their formidable display would strike terror to the opposing ranks, but when they heard the Major's reply and saw his men ready to execute it, it filled them with consternation, and they struck an air-line for the nearest woods. The Major's men took a circuitous route and intercepted them while passing a ravine about two miles from the scene of battle. They at once fired upon the marauders, and their rout became gen- eral. The only life lost was that of the constable's horse, which fell at the first fire, giving its owner a lift in the world he had not calculated on, and landing him in a bunch of brambles. Out of this he crawled, minus hat and gun, and struck the very fastest gait he could on a bee-line for New Jersey, each particular hair stand- ing so straight behind that it was said a pick-axe could have been hung upon it and not have fallen off. The victory was complete; and thus in the second regular engagement did the Jerseymen return home worsted.

The next raid of the Jerseymen took place in 1753, and was made to obtain possession of the lands and person of Thomas De Key (or Dekay), who was at that time Colonel of the Orange county militia, and also justice of the peace. De Key, wishing to get along without any disturbance, went to James Alexander, one of the proprietors of East New Jersey, and asked to remain unmolested till the boundary should be determined. This Alexander would not agree to, stating that the land belonged to New Jersey, and that he must submit to the laws of that State. This the Colonel in turn refused to do, and so the question remained. Shortly after, a party of armed men from New Jersey appeared before the Colonel's door. He had perceived them approaching, and had prepared for defense by arming himself and stoutly barricading all the entrances to the house. He then appeared at a window and warned them that death awaited the first man who should undertake to force an entrance to the house. This rather checkmated their plans. Some of them cocked their guns and threatened to shoot the Colonel through the heart as he stood at the window—others swearing they would set fire to the house and shoot every man, woman and child, that should undertake to flee from it; and some declaring in favor of starving him out. But Colonel De Key was not so easily intimidated. He stuck to his position, and the enemy again were forced to retire, vowing that next time they would bring a force with them large enough to take the whole of Goshen, and assuring the Colonel that they would have him yet.

The matter was frequently brought before the Colonial Assemblies of both New York and New Jersey, by the proprietors of the Minisink and Wawayanada patents, and in 1754 Lieut. Gov. James De Lancey noticed it in the following message to that body in New York:

" *Gentlemen*—The division line between this govern-

ment and the province of New Jersey not being settled,
has given rise to great tumults and disorders among the
people of Orange County and the adjacent inhabitants
of New Jersey, and may produce worse evils unless prevented by a timely care. Nothing can answer the purpose so effectually, I think, as the fixing of a temporary
line of peace between us, until his Majesty's pleasure
shall be known in the matter. Governer Belcher assures
me of his sincere desire that amicable and conciliatory
measures may be fallen upon by the governments to
make the borders easy: and I have proposed to him the
running such line conformable' to the opinion of his
Majesty's council, signified in their report to me, which
I shall order to be laid before you, and if it receives
your approbation I shall forthwith appoint commissioners
for running such line of peace, and apply to that government to do the like on their part."

But notwithstanding the above message promised to
so speedily provide for the welfare of the people of Minisink by a settlement of this vexatious question, it was
not heard of again for years, and the quarrel continued.
About 1765 the last raid of the Jerseymen took place,
for the capture of Major and Johannes Westbrook—two
persons who lived within the limits of the disputed territory, and were leading men in the ranks of the Minisink claimants. The invaders chose Sunday for the
accomplishment of their design, and resolved to falsify
the old proverb that " Evil men love darkness rather
than light," by making the venture in broad daylight.
The appointed day came. The Major and Captain
Westbrook as usual attended the Maghackemeck Church,
to listen to the expounding of divine writ by Mr. Thomas
Romeyn, the pastor. The psalms were sung, the prayers
made, and the minister went on with his discourse.

Little thought his hearers as they waxed drowsy with the length of the good man's sermon and the warmth of the day, that a far more exciting topic than his every-day struggle in wordy combat with the powers of dark-ness, awaited their consideration; that even while they suffered their thoughts to stray from the text to the satisfy-ing consolation of a good Sunday dinner, a circle of dark forms was drawing closer and closer around the edifice. The services closed. It was a direful moment. The Major and Captain Westbrook appeared, and the be-siegers rushed toward them with a shout. But quick as were their movements, those of the attacked were quicker. Hats and coats were doffed—shouts of defi-ance arose—positions of defence assumed on the instant, and the attackers met with stubborn resistance. Neither party violated the sanctity of the Sabbath by the use of arms other than those given by nature. The women screamed, cried and scolded—the men shouted, fought, and no doubt thought of some very profane words, if they did not speak them. The place which a few moments before was a perfect pattern of Sabbath quietness, was changed as if by the enchanter's wand into a complete pandemonium. Frightful sounds of discord, kicks, cuffs, blows and maddened yells of victory or pain, mingled with the tones of entreaty, sobs and screams, filled the air. The green was covered with the crowd of terrified women and maddened, struggling men.

"Long time in even scale the battle hung."

Down and up, and over and under they went as the tide of battle turned. The faces so contented and serene while the minister was fighting evil doers with the Scriptures, now began to present a motley array of bloody noses, blackened eyes, and lips cut and swollen, since they had grappled with the powers of New Jersey.

3*

But why prolong the description of this unequal contest?
The Jerseymen in this instance proved too numerous
for the Minisinkers, and marched off the Major and
Captain in triumph. The prisoners, however, without
doubt, consoled themselves somewhat with the thought
that they had at least made their capture a "lively
time" for their assailants. They were confined some
time in what was called the Jersey Colony prison, but
finally released.

Thus this hard-fought battle of the fist was at last
productive of barren results. This was the last signal
engagement of the war. The governments of the two
Colonies in 1767 appointed Commissioners to run a
boundary line, but such was the bitterness of feeling
among the inhabitants that they dared not do it, and as
a reason for not performing their duty, stated in their
report that the Indians were so hostile they deemed it
unsafe. The line was shortly after surveyed however,
the disputed territory about equally divided between
the claimants—and so the war was peaceably settled at
last, just as it might have been at first, if the ruling
powers had been composed of men desirous of doing so.

CHAPTER V.

The two governments, France and England, could not fail of being jealous of each other, rivals as they were for the mastery of the western continent ; and this feeling found vent in a continued series of predatory excursions into each other's colonial possessions, and divers strategical efforts to gain the ascendancy in a favorable alliance with the warlike tribes of Indians. Especially was this the case along the borders of the Canadas and the province of New York and those of New England. It was this spirit of hatred and jealousy among the Indians, fostered and encouraged on the one side by the English against the French, and on the other by the French against the English, that caused such a long record of horrible atrocities to be connected with the Indian name in the early history of the Colonies. But though for many years the tide of war had vacillated between the opposing parties with undecisive results to either side, its bloody front had not as yet shown itself in a serious form among the settlers of the Minisink region ; and it was not till 1754 that they began to perceive signs of an approaching tempest. During that year England directed the Colonies to oppose the encroachments of the French by force of arms, though the mother countries were at peace with each other. The war gradually increased, and the following year became a general contest between the two nations, and has been ever since known in history as the " old French and Indian war of 1755."

The struggle was entered upon with the determination to throw all possible force into the scale. In February of that year, the legislature of New York voted 45,000 pounds sterling to defray expenses, and in May ordered a levy of 800 men to be made to co-operate with the troops of the other Colonies. The most stringent measures were adopted to secure the public safety; and among others equally severe, was a law passed the same year by the legislature, to the effect that in cases of imminent danger, slaves were liable to military duty, and that if any colored person over the age of fourteen was found a mile or more from his or her master's plantation, without a certificate from the master stating their business, they were to be judged guilty of felony, without benefit of clergy. The same law also declared that any person so finding a slave or slaves had the right to shoot or destroy him or them without being liable to impeachment or prosecution for the same.

The first intimation the Minisink settlers had of approaching danger, was the disappearance of the Indians from their neighborhood. Squads of them that had been on the most friendly terms with the whites were suddenly missed, and the few Indians that remained told them that they had gone to join the hostile tribes near Cochecton and farther west. The settlers knew enough of Indian character to foresee the ordeal to which they were to be subjected, and began to prepare for the worst. The women and children were first sent to a place of safety—to Old Paltz, Rochester, and Wawarsing in Ulster county, and to Goshen in Orange, at all of which places the majority of them had relatives

by marriage or otherwise ; for they knew the fury of
the Indian would be vented alike on the strong and the
helpless. Though their vicinity had hitherto been
spared, the terrible details of Indian vengeance as seen
in the murder at Schaghticoke were fresh in their
memory.

Capt. Johannis Bratt and David Ketlin were two
pioneers in the wilderness, at a place called by the
Indians Schaghticoke, near Albany. For companionship
they built their houses a short distance apart, and
many a long day in this lonely place the only sound
heard by either to enliven his toil, was the echo of the
other's axe amid the mighty timber. Time enabled
them to surround themselves with many comforts, and
Indian depredations so frequent in the surrounding
country had been a thing unknown to them, except by
rumor, which never failed to tell them of horrible crimes
committed, whenever they went to Albany for necessaries. But they had done nothing to incur the resent-
ment of the red man, and so they trusted in Providence
and toiled on. On the 20th of October, 1711, they
started from their homes to visit a settlement distant
some two miles—Ketlin on foot and Bratt on horseback.
They had proceeded but a short distance, when they
met an Indian sauntering along with his gun upon his
shoulder. Ketlin spoke to him in the Indian language,
and asked where he was going. He replied that he
was going a hunting. "But," said Ketlin, "where are
your comrades?" He answered, "They have gone
ahead into the woods." Ketlin turned to Capt. Bratt,
remarking in Dutch that there was something suspicious
about his actions, and that he was a strange Indian.
The instant Ketlin turned to speak to the Captain, the
Indian slung his rifle to his shoulder and fired, killing

the Captain dead upon his horse. The suddenness of
the terrific act, for a moment paralyzed Ketlin's
thoughts, but it was for a moment only. He knew that
his own life depended on the quickness of his movements, and sprang at once to grapple with his foe, as
he had no weapons of any kind. The Indian had drawn
his tomahawk, or rather axe, and as Ketlin approached
struck a murderous blow at his head ; but he dodged
it, and scarcely too, for the helve hit his shoulder.
Then came the struggle for life. Ketlin was a powerful
man, and desperation lent him new strength. It was
an anxious moment, that comprehended the period of
that trial of strength on foot ; but Ketlin was the
superior and succeeded in throwing his antagonist. In
the fall he was also fortunate enough to secure the axe
in his left hand. The Indian saw that he was gaining
the advantage, but like his tribe, it only seemed to
increase his courage.

"You shall die," he hissed between his set teeth.
"There are twenty French Indians on both sides the
river."

"That may be," said Ketlin, "but you will die first."

To carry out the threat, he undertook to change the
axe from his left hand to his right. At that instant the
Indian, concentrating all his energies, gave him a tremendous heave. It displaced him somewhat, and ere
he could recover his advantage the Indian gained his
feet, broke from his grasp, and with a yell of triumph disappeared in the forest. He started to pursue him, but
a vine caught his foot and threw him violently to the
ground. Ketlin brought the Indian's gun and axe home
and then went to the settlement and notified the inhabitants of the struggle. Capt. Bratt's body was brought
to Albany the same day. Knowing the habits of Indian

warfare, it was reasonable to suppose that they would seek revenge that night. Ketlin therefore procured the services of three soldiers and proceeded to prepare his house for defense. The little garrison consisted of Ketlin's family, his brother's wife and two children, the three soldiers, and an Indian boy.

The evening wore away in silence. Hours passed slowly to the fearful minds of the watchful ones in that lonely house, and still no signs of the enemy. About midnight a timid knock was heard upon the door. Ketlin asked in the Indian tongue who was there. An Indian voice answered, " It is I.".

" Where do you come from ?" asked Ketlin.

" From the other side of the river. I am a friend and wish to help you against the French Indians. Open the door."

" I am afraid you will cheat me," said Ketlin.

" No," replied the Indian, " I'm a friend ; open the door."

A hurried consultation was held by the inmates, and almost all opposed it. But Ketlin declared that if a friend they needed his help, and if an enemy they could very easily keep him out. Suiting his action to his opinion, he fearlessly stepped to the door and swung it partly open. Dearly did he pay for his temerity. Instantly there was a blinding flash of light, a deafening report, and he fell dead, pierced by six musket balls. A moment's silence, and then the whole forest seemed alive with the whooping demons. The soldiers fired a volley at the dusky forms of the advancing savages; it checked them, and Ketlin's son, a boy of sixteen, sprang up and closed the door. The women loaded the rifles, and handed the ammunition to the heroic defenders of that ill-starred house. Long they kept the enemy at

bay by firing from the port-holes and windows, but it
was doomed to be all in vain. A low spluttering sound
kept rising higher and higher, till at last it made itself
heard above the crack of the rifles and the yells of the
savage foe. A kind of yellow twilight began to light up
the forest. The beseiged gathered around the dead
body of their friend, husband and father, and debated
as to the last chance they had of saving themselves.
The savages were silent now—their success was certain.
The house was on fire. Nothing now disturbed the
stillness of the night, save the increasing roar of the
crackling flames. The coals began to fall through the
floor overhead, and the inmates knew they could stay
in the house no longer. A brief prayer was breathed;
they grasped each other's hand in a mute farewell, for
well they knew they would never all meet together again
until they gained the shores of the unknown world of
eternity. Then one of the soldiers opened the door and
cried "Now !" and they all sprang for their lives. The
soldiers were ahead. The first one was shot dead; the
next was pursued and taken prisoner, and the third one
shot. The next was the Indian boy, who was shot
through the arm and breast, but succeeded in getting to
the woods and escaped. Ketlin's son kept firing till he
was at last shot through the shoulder and taken prisoner. The women and children were made prisoners.
Fire was applied to the barns, and the whole party then
started away. About a quarter of a mile from the
house, Ketlin's wife being in a very delicate situation,
was so overcome by fright that she sank down by the
path. Seeing she could proceed no farther, one of the
savages bared her throat across a small log. She made
no complaint, but folding her hands over her breast,
closed her eyes, and met her doom without a sigh. A

moment the tomahawk was poised in the air, and as the light from her burning home lighted up her bare throat, it descended swiftly and her head was almost severed from her body. Then grasping the hair of her head in one hand, he dexterously drew the scalping-knife in the other, and running a gash around the scalp tore it off with a sudden wrench, swung aloft his bloody trophy with a whoop, and rejoined his comrades.

The other woman had a young child she carried in her arms. Shortly after the murder of Ketlin's wife it began to cry, and all its mother's efforts to keep it quiet were unavailing. Angry at its noise, one of the savages seized it by the heels, tore it from its mother's arms, swung it out at arms' length and dashed its brains out against an oak tree. At the fate of her infant, the mother uttered a heart-piercing cry. It was her last. In an instant the murderous tomahawk had sank into her brain, and the next moment her form lay upon the ground, a scalpless, quivering corpse.

All that returned to tell the tale was the Indian boy who escaped from the burning house. The other particulars were learned from an old lame Indian who happened in the vicinity and followed the retreating party. (Vol. v. p. 281 Doc. relating to N. Y.)

This incident is given, not because it was remembered more by the people of Minisink than others of the kind, but because it more fully illustrates the leading traits of Indian character—duplicity, cunning and revenge. No wonder was it that the inhabitants of the Minisink Region betook themselves to measures of defense at the first alarm. Some of their bravest men had volunteered to fight against the French, and the people of the Peenpack neighborhood had furnished the great northern expedition with a team, wagon, and teamster,

Three forts were built in what was known as the upper
neighborhood (or Peenpack), and three in the lower
neighborhood next the Delaware river. Those in Peenpack were located, one on the Neversink at the north-
west end of the settlement, not far from where Cuddebackville now stands; one at the house of Peter Gumaer,
in the central part of the neighborhood; and one in the
southwest of the settlement, at the house of Mr. Westfall, near the farm lately occupied by Peter Swartout,
Esq. These three forts gave protection to about twelve
families. The location of the three forts in the lower
neighborhood is not precisely known, no record of them
being preserved. They are said to have afforded protection to about eighteen families.

The first incident that showed the people of this
region how well-timed were their precautions, occurred
about the time of harvest in the year 1756. Three men
in the lower neighborhood went out one morning to
commence cutting a field of grain. As usual they took
their guns along, not thinking however of seeing any
Indians, as nothing had been heard of any in the vicinity.
Arriving at the field they set down their guns and commenced work. While working along busily they got
some distance from their arms, and were suddenly start-
led by the dread warwhoop. A glance showed them
their peril. A party of Indians had been lying in
ambush and had seized their guns. They ran for their
lives, but the Indians' aim was unerring. They were all
three killed, and their scalpless bodies found soon after.
Pursuit was given, but in vain; the spoilers were too
wary to be overtaken.

At another time a band of Indians made an effort to
capture the fort at Westfall's, and came near being
successful. They sent out a couple of scouts, who dis-

covered the fort to be occupied by two women only. As soon as this intelligence reached the main body they made instant preparations for its capture. But luckily, in the interval a party of soldiers going from New Jersey to Esopus came along, and stopped at the fort for refreshments. Not knowing this, the Indians suddenly burst in the doors before the soldiers were fairly seated. They were somewhat surprised at the unexpected presence of the soldiers, but nothing daunted, they fired a volley at them and then throwing aside their guns fell upon them with the tomahawk. The soldiers retreated to the chamber of the building, and recovering from the first panic, they opened such a deadly fire upon the intruders that they were soon forced to vacate the premises. This was a closely contested battle and cost the lives of several of the soldiers as well as a goodly number of the Indians.

But the settlers were not always successful in these contests. A large party of Indians during one of their forays into the settlement, attacked the upper fort on the Neversink. It was well garrisoned, and its defenders made a brave resistance. One savage after another fell before the aim of the beseiged, and they would soon have had to give up the attack had not the fort taken fire from the burning of the barn near by. The heat soon became so intense that the inmates were forced to the alternative of risking their chances by flight or perishing in the flames. There was not much difference in the modes of death, and both were certain. As the flames enveloped the building, one after another stole from the death by fire, only to meet a more speedy one by the bullet or tomahawk. Not a single man of the garrison escaped. The only women in the fort, the Captain's wife and a colored woman, secreted them-

selves in the cellar. Here they remained till the coals
began to fall through the floor, when the white woman
ran out and endeavored to elude pursuit by running
round the house. The Indians followed her in a body,
and soon overtook and killed her. When the shout of
victory that announced the death of the Captain's wife,
reached the ears of the black woman, she rightly judged
it a proper time to make a trial for life ; and accordingly
ran under the shadow of the smoke for the nearest
woods. The savages being on the other side of the
fort did not perceive her, and she gained the covert of
the timber in safety. She then concealed herself on
the banks of the Neversink till morning, when she took
a circuitous route through the woods to Gumaer's fort,
the sole survivor of the massacre. The Captain came
home a day or two afterwards, and then learned for the
first time the tidings of the sad catastrophe. The
friends, the comfortable home, the loving wife—all he
had but a short time before left so happy and cheerful—
were gone ! Nothing remained to tell of their existence
but the smoldering ashes of the fort and the disfigured
corpses of its occupants. By the grave of his wife he
took an oath of vengeance ; and during the remaining
years of his life, many a red-skin was sent to the world
of spirits by his hand, in redemption of the pledge.

There was an incident connected with the capture of
this fort, that for a long time was held by the super-
stitious people of the neighborhood as a singular fatality.
Two women from Gumaer's fort had been there visiting
on the day of the attack. During their visit the soldiers
had been telling stories and jokes, and getting the " rig"
on different ones as usual. Among other things they
told the colored woman they were going to be attacked
by the Indians soon, and that she need not expect to

escape for she was too fat to run fast. The result was altogether different from their prophecy. The attack came sooner than they dreamt of, and she was the only one that did escape.

Whenever one of the settlers wished to visit his relatives at Goshen, or in Napanoch, it was always necessary to take along an escort of soldiers, or to travel in companies, so beset were the roads with lurking savages. Abraham Low and William Cuddeback, on one occasion undertook a journey to Rochester, Ulster county, alone in a wagon. On the return route, near home, they were shot at by Indians concealed near the roadside. Low was wounded in the shoulder, but by applying the whip vigorously, the horse soon carried them out of danger.

A man named Owens, was soon after killed while at work in the meadow of Asa Dolsen, by a strolling band of Indians. Dolsen immediately removed his family to Goshen for safety. The scene of this incident was in what is known as Dolsentown, in the north-eastern part of the present town of Wawayanda.

Near the same place, three Indians, on another occasion, chased a man for a long distance. At last he crept under some weeds and brush at the foot of a tree which had blown down. The Indians came and stood upon the body of the tree, and after looking around for some time gave two or three yells and departed, without discovering the object of their search who was so near them.

Two brothers, Daniel and David Cooley, had located on farms near Mr. Dolsen's. In those days it was customary to build ovens separate from the houses. David Cooley's wife one day was going from the oven to the house, just as a party of Indians were passing. Without a word one of them leveled his rifle and shot her dead. This cold-blooded deed was perpetrated on the farm now owned by the heirs of Capt. John Cummings.

East of this the Indians seldom ventured; though one Sunday morning a man by the name of Webb was killed by them, just over the outlet in the town of Goshen. This they boasted of a great deal, but their operations were mostly confined to petty thefts in that quarter, owing to the thickness of the settlements.

During this war an incident occurred in the Minisink settlement that forms a striking illustration of the force of attachment to the savage mode of life. A straggling band of Indians captured a little son of Mr. Westfall's, near the fort at the north-west end of the Peenpack settlement, in the commencement of the war. Nothing more was heard of him for years. The French and Indian war with its train of horrors and barbarities became a thing of the past. Still no tidings came to the parents of the absent one, whom they had long mourned as dead. The Revolutionary war with its red waves of savage desolation swept over the land, and still nought came to tell the parents of a different fate for the loved and lost. Finally the father died. By some means the son, who was still living in a far off Indian home, obtained intelligence of his death, and came back to the settlement with an interpreter to get possession of his inheritance. He was taken to the farm where his father had lived and where he had been taken prisoner, but had no recollection of the premises, except a small pond of water near the house where he was playing when captured. His mother recognized him in spite of his Indian garb and broad Indian tongue. She endeavored by maternal feelings, pecuniary considerations, and personal appeals, to induce him to remain and live with her during the few remaining years of her life. But so attached was he to his life in the wilderness that he refused to listen to any project of the kind. He obtained his share of his father's estate, bade his mother good bye, turned his back on everything that could conduce to the enjoyment of civilized life, and was soon trudging away in the forest to his Indian home and bride.

The contest between England and France that gave rise to such horrible atrocities as those recorded in this chapter, and which may be considered a fair sample of similar occurrences everywhere along the border of the American provinces, was finally ended by the triumph of the British Colonial armies; and the fall of Montreal and Quebec reduced the French Canadian possessions to complete submission to the authority of the British crown.

CHAPTER VI.

The conclusion of the old " French and Indian war " as it was termed, gave to the settlers a number of years of peace, excepting an occasional petty theft or outrage by a wandering party of Indians. The work of reclaiming the fertile land to a state of cultivation again went forward. The wives and children of the inhabitants ventured to return again to their old homes, from the distant villages whither they had fled to escape the Indian's hate. New comers began to flock to the fertile hills and vales of the Minisink Region and of western Orange, and prosperity again smiled upon the efforts of the hardy pioneer.

But just at this time, when everything bid fair for a long season of quietness, the arbitrary acts of England, under whose banner they had faced death a thousand times in sanguinary struggles with the savage foe, or in fighting the French beneath the walls of Montreal and Quebec, began to arouse within their breasts a desire to be free. Instead of trying to allay this feeling of discontent by measures calculated to satisfy the public mind; England each succeeding year appeared to be seeking new methods of taxation, and as a consequence the desire for a release from her power became a necessity. This necessity was not long in manifesting its resistance to odious acts of the Crown by force. Organized measures for defense were adopted by the provinces, and thus began the great Revolutionary struggle. The Continental Congress took possession of the affairs of the colonies, and began to direct the resisting forces. But it was soon found that many persons throughout the provinces were determined to sustain the British government. Meetings were held in different places to give the new Congress proof of the people's approval of their acts. The principal of these was held in the city of New York on the 29th of April, 1775.

In order to form a distinction between the friends of liberty and its foes, and to prevent anarchy as far as possible, it was resolved to form an association in each county throughout the thirteen Colonies. This was done by transmitting to each county a pledge which every friend of the new movement was expected to sign. This at once drew the dividing line between the Whigs and Tories. It embittered the feeling greatly between them, for those that refused to affix their names to it were marked men. All honor to the signers of that document! Each name, if possible, should be rendered imperishable. Every one realizing the benefits of the glorious Temple of Liberty, of the mild and beneficent laws, and enduring principles of government reared by their efforts, should ever think of them with gratitude. Their names are more worthy of immortality than those of Alexander or Cæsar. Many of their descendants still reside in Orange county, and well may they point with pride to the glorious record their ancestors have left behind them. The following is a copy of the pledge, taken from Eager's History:

PLEDGE OF 1775.

" Persuaded that the salvation of the rights and liber-
4

ties of America depend, under God, on the firm union of
its inhabitants in a rigorous prosecution of the measures
necessary for its safety; and convinced of the necessity
of preventing anarchy and confusion, which attend the
dissolution of the powers of government, we, the free-
men, freeholders, and inhabitants of Orange County,
New York, being greatly alarmed at the avowed design
of the Ministry to raise a revenue in America, and
shocked by the bloody scene now acting in Massachusetts
Bay, do, in the most solemn manner, resolve never to
become slaves ; and do associate, under all the ties of
religion, honor and love to our country, to adopt and
endeavor to carry into execution whatever measures
may be recommended by the Continental Congress or
resolved upon by our Provincial Convention for the
purpose of preserving our constitution and opposing the
execution of the several arbitrary Acts of the British
Parliament, until a reconciliation between Great Brit-
tain and America on constitutional principles (which
we most ardently desire,) can be obtained; and that we
will in all things follow the advice of our general committee respecting the purposes aforesaid, the preservation of peace and good order, and the safety of individuals and property."

NAMES OF THE SIGNERS OF THE ABOVE, FROM THE PRESENT TOWN OF DEER.
PARK (THEN A PART OF THE TOWN OF MAMAKATING.
ULSTER CO.,) JUNE 26, 1775.

John Young,	John Stufflebane,
Philip Swartout, Esq.,	John Stufflebane, Jr.,
Benjamin Depue,	James Blizard,
Capt. John Crage,	Thomas Combs,
William Haxton,	James McCivers,
John McKinstry,	Joseph Hubbard,
Benj. Cuddeback, Jr.,	John Thompson,
Robert Cook,	Ebenezer Halcomb,

Harmanus Van Inwegen,
T. K. Westbrook,
William Rose,
Samuel Depue,
William Johnston,
James Williams,
Charles Gillets,
Eli Strickland,
David Gillaspy,
Stephen Larney,
Capt. J. R. Dewitt,
Abr. Cuddeback, Jr.,
Samuel King,
Abna Skinner,
Fred. Benaer,
Valentine Wheeler,
Thomas Kytte,
Jonathan Brooks,
John Wallis,
Joseph Drake,
Ebenezer Parks,
Jacobus Swartout,
Gerardus Swartout,
Phil. Swartout, Jr.,
Isaac Van Twill,
Joseph Westfork,
Petrus Gumaer,
J. DeWitt Gumaer,
Daniel Van Fleet, Jr.,
Ezekiel Gumore,
Jacob Van Inaway,
Moses Depue, Jr.,
Jacobus Cuddeback,
Rufus Stanton,

G. Van Inwegen,
Wm. Cuddeback,
Abr. Cuddeback,
Eliphalet Stevens,
Elisha Travis,
Albert Rosa,
Adam Rivenburg,
Mathew Neely,
Samuel Dealy,
William Smith,
John Harding,
Nathan Cook,
Jep. Fuller,
Eph. Thomas,
. Henry Elsworth,
Joseph Thomas,
Abr. M'Quin,
John Seybolt,
Joseph Skinner,
Joseph Arthur,
David Wheeler,
John Travis,
John Travis, Jr.,
Daniel Decker,
Petrus Cuddeback,
Elias Gumore,
John Brooks,
Elisha Barber,
Jonathan Davis,
Robert Comfort,
David Daly,
Gershom Simpson,
Eph. Forgisson,
Jacob Comfort,

Reuben Babbett,
Jonathan Wheeler,
Asa Kimball,
Robert Milliken,
Thomas Lake,
Zeh. Holcomb,
John Williams,
John Stry,
Joel Adams,
Joseph Shaw,
George Gillaspy,
James Cumen,
Abraham Rosa,
Jacob Rosa,
Henry Newkirk,
Peter Simpson,
Stephen Holcomb,
Johannes Miller,
Daniel Woodworth,
Moses Roberts,
Daniel Roberts,
John Douglass,
Joseph Randall,

Jacob Stanton,
Moses Miller,
Jonah Parks,
John Gillaspy,
Jno. Barber,
Samuel Patterson,
Abraham Smedes,
Nathaniel Travis,
Ezekiel Travis,
Joseph Travis,
Thos. Gillaspy,
Jeremiah Shaver.
Joseph Ogden,
Daniel Walling.
Daniel Walling, Jr.,
Elias Miller,
Isaac Roosa,
Abr. Smith,
George G. Denniston,
Mathew Terwilleger.
Leonard Hefinessy,
Jonathan Strickland,
Johannes Wash.

NAMES OF THE SIGNERS FROM THE OLD TOWN OF MINISINK, (NOW DIVIDED
INTO MINISINK, MOUNT HOPE, WAWAYANDA AND GREENVILLE.)

J. Westbrook, Jr.,
Wilhelmus Westfall,
Johannes Decker, Jr.,
Benjamin Cox,
Moses Cortright,   •
Jacob Quick,
John Prys,
Jacobus Harraken,
Timothy Wood,

Nicholas Slyter,
James Carpenter,
Reuben Jones,
Daniel St. John.
Esee Bronson,
Petrus Cole,
Aldert Osterhoudt,
Isaac Uptegrove,
A. Van Etten,

Benjamin Wood,
Levi Decker,
G. Braddock,
Samuel Davis,
Martinas Decker,
Petrus Cuykendal,
Isaac Davis,
Benjamin Boorman,
Sylvester Cortright,
George Quick,
Nehemiah Patterson,
Jacobus Schoonhoven,
Jacobus Davis,
Asa Astley,
Benjamin Corsan,
Martinas Decker, Jr.,
Ephraim Middaugh,
Johannes Westbrook,
Solomon Cuykendal,
John Bennet,
Simon Westfall,
Arthur Van Tile,
Jacobus Vanfliet, Jr.,
Jacobus Vanfliet,
Wilhelmus Cole,
Thomas Hart,
Levi Van Etten,
Petrus Decker,
John Van Tuyle,
Daniel Cole,
S. Cuykendal, Jr.,
Daniel Kortright,
Joel Westbrook,
A. C. Van Akin.

The names of those who did not sign the pledge are not recorded, and it is as well that they should be suffered to rest in oblivion; for mankind at the present day can form but very imperfect decisions on the motives which may have influenced the actions of men a hundred years ago. The number of non-signers, or Tories, as they were called, was far greater in the eastern than in the western part of Orange county. The present town of Deerpark (then a part of Mamakating, Ulster county,) was unanimous in support of the measure; John Young, chairman of the committee, reporting it to have been signed by every householder within the limits of the town.

CHAPTER VII.

The commencement of the Revolutionary struggle at once opened to the view of the colonists the magnitude of the great undertaking upon which they had entered. They saw that in addition to the armies and munitions of war it would be necessary to oppose to the power and discipline of Great Britain, that an enemy lurked upon their own soil that required full as much energy and watchfulness to circumvent as the troopers of old King George. They saw many of their neighbors openly espouse the cause of royalty, some of whom departed at once and sought a place in the ranks of the king's myrmidons as open foes, while others, less honorable, remained behind to furnish information to the invaders of their country, and to stimulate the scattering Indians to deeds of atrocity against their former friends that have sullied the otherwise fair page of American history, and associated the names of the Indian and Tory with the blackest scenes of horror and cruelty that the world has ever seen. The eastern part of Orange county was more infected with Tory principles than the western; and it was fortunate that it was so, for the mountain ravines and straggling Indian parties that infested them in the Minisink Region, furnished the material which, with a little more Royalist help, would have turned the settlement into barren ruins, and which as it was, made it the theatre of the bloodiest acts of the war. The Indians, during the struggles that had taken place previously, had imbibed a hatred of the whites that required but a few presents and assurances of help to at once enlist on the Royalist's side against the rebels. This they did in violation of a treaty which General Schuyler on the part of Congress had concluded with the Six Nations of western New York, in July, 1775, by which they were to observe strict neutrality between the Americans and British. This, however, was opposed to Indian philosophy; and it was not long before the British induced them to break their pledges. At first the Indians singled out persons as the objects of attack against whom they had some particular animosity or whom they feared; but during the progress of the war they collected together in large bodies, and in conjunction with the Tories carried on a more wholesale scheme of murder. The father of the famous Tom Quick fell a victim to Indian ferocity in the south of the Minisink Region, during the old French war, and the circumstances of his death aroused such a feeling of animosity against the Indians in the breast of Tom Quick, that he determined to devote his whole life to purposes of revenge. He led a sort of wandering life, intent on one single object—the killing of every Indian that came in his way, and so well did he fulfill his pledge, that to this day the name of " Tom Quick, the Indian slayer," is a household word in the vicinity of the Minisink Region. He was never married. The history of his exploits now forms the subject of a volume, greatly interesting to those who delight to review the light and dark scenes of pioneer life a hundred years ago. His greatest exploits took place during and after the Revolution.

The grandfather of Mr. Nathaniel R. Quick, at present a resident of the town of Greenville, was also much feared by the Indians. On one occasion they laid an ambush for him in a desolate part of the path leading to his house. He had been out hunting, and when he was returning he was suddenly surprised as he came near this place by seeing an Indian spring into the path ahead of him. The Indian at the same instant brought his rifle to his shoulder and fired at him; but being in too great a hurry fortunately missed him, though the bullet passed alarmingly close to his head. Seeing but one Indian he immediately shot him. At the same moment another bullet whistled by his shoulders, and finding it to be getting dangerous he at once darted off on a race for life. The Indians pursued him some distance and fired at him several times. One bullet struck him in the side, inflicting a severe flesh wound, but otherwise he escaped unhurt.

In 1777 they attacked the family of a Mr. Sprague, a resident of the northern part of the settlement, and took some of them prisoners.

The family of a Mr. Brooks was next attacked, and several killed. The rest were taken prisoners.

These deeds awoke the Minisink people to a sense of their situation. Many of their bravest men were absent doing duty in distant parts of the State as soldiers. Capt. Cuddeback, Gerardus Swartout, Cornelius Swartout and Gerardus Van Inwegen, on whose exertions they had formerly chiefly relied for protection, had been on service at Fort Montgomery, and were there when it was captured by the British, Oct. 6, 1777. At the time of the attack, Capt. Cuddeback was sent across the Hudson with a party of men to prevent the British from cutting the chain which was stretched across the river opposite the fort. Thus he escaped being in tho battle. Van Inwegen and the Swartouts remained in the fort. The Swartouts escaped during the surrender of the fort, but Van Inwegen was killed in the assault. The absence of these men was severely felt by the people of Minisink, but they bravely determined to prove themselves possessed of the same spirit. In 1778 a committee of safety was appointed for the settlement. The first committee was Benjamin DuPuy, Philip Swartout, and Thomas Kytte. Harmanus Van Inwegen was admitted as a member afterwards. They at once ordered the erection or repairing of the forts at the houses of Jacob Rutson DeWitt, Benjamin DuPuy and Ezekiel Gumaer, in the Peenpack neighborhood; one at the house of Maj. John Decker, and one at the house of Daniel Van Auken in the lower neighborhood. They also sent many women and children to the older settlements, as the forts could not accommodate the whole fifty families which at that time inhabited what is now the town of Deerpark. Scouting parties were also instituted under command of Capt. Bezaliel Tyler, who scouted the woods as far west as Cochecton, where a few families resided. Persons suspected of aiding the Indians were imprisoned or banished from the region. Through their intercession small parties of nine months militia were obtained to garrison the forts. These preparations were hardly fairly begun before their wisdom and propriety became apparent by the

MASSACRE OF WYOMING.

Wyoming was the name of a pleasant settlement on both sides of the Susquehanna river in the northern

part of Pennsylvania. The fertility of its soil and its
beautiful location in the midst of a smiling valley, invi-
ted hundreds from different parts of Orange and Ulster
counties and the Minisink Region, to take up a residence
within its limits. No where else had they found so de-
sirable a spot for a home as on the banks of the noble
Susquehanna in that quiet valley. No settlement had
been so prosperous, and in 1778 it numbered a population of eleven hundred families. They were partriotic,
too, those settlers of Wyoming, for at roll-call in the
morning ten hundred of their sons, and brothers, and
husbands, answered to their names in the Continental
army. No wonder was it that this feeling should induce
them to treat rather harshly the few Tories in their
midst whom they saw plotting with the Indians against
their friends in the army. The Tories had long sought
for an opportunity of open rupture, and they now allied
themselves with the Indians and swore revenge. Their
time was favorable, for the flower of the Wyoming
youth were in the American army. The settlers,
aware of their insecurity, erected four forts upon different points of the settlement, among which they dis-
tributed about five hundred men; the whole under
command of Colonel Zebulon Butler, a cousin of John,
the celebrated Tory. (Zebulon was afterward accused
of treachery, but capacity was undoubtedly what he
most stood in need of.) This done, the settlers wrote
to Washington praying for immediate assistance, for a
presentiment of their approaching fate seemed to per-
vade their minds in spite of the assurances of friendship
which the Indians were continually pouring into their
ears. Their messages were intercepted by the Pennsylvania loyalists, but at all events they would have
been too late. The savages had already appeared upon

the frontiers of the settlement, and the cruelties they were perpetrating were frightful; the mournful prelude to those more terrible scenes which were shortly to follow.

About the commencement of the month of July, the Indians suddenly appeared in strong force upon the banks of the Susquehanna. They numbered about 1,600 men, from four to six hundred of them pure Indians, and the rest Tories disguised and painted to resemble them. They were commanded by Col. Brandt, a half-breed, and John Butler; both renowned for their ferocity in previous expeditions. One of the forts, nearest the border, surrendered at the first approach of the enemy, owing to treachery in the garrison. The next fort was defended successfully for a time, but the enemy assaulted it so vigorously that the garrison was finally forced to surrender at discretion. The victors spared the women and children, but the rest were butchered without mercy. Zebulon then withdrew with his forces into the principal fort, called Kingston. Upon this fortification the settlers had placed their main reliance, being the largest and strongest of the four. All who were unable to bear arms—the sick, women and children, and old men—repaired thither in throngs, weeping and uttering despairing cries, as the last place of refuge which could be defended with any hope of success. On came the long irregular line of the enemy, shouting and yelling like so many demons. Zebulon disposed of the troops in the garrison to the best advantage possible and awaited the coming foe. It was evident the settlers had it in their power if attacked to make the assaulting party pay dearly for their temerity. Brandt saw this, and commanded his forces to halt before coming within gunshot. The cunning half-breed then sent John Butler to hold a

parley with his cousin Zebulon, hoping that the ties of
relationship might lead Zebulon to place confidence in
the artful story of the Tory. Nor was he mistaken.
John was lavish of promises, and succeeded in making
Zebulon believe that if he would consent to a parley in
the open field the matter could easily be settled and the
siege raised.   The next morning, in accordance with
his pledge, John Butler had retired with his forces, and
the settlers looked from the walls of the fort over the
valley without seeing an Indian.   This was a gladsome
relief, and they at once proceeded to fulfill their part of
the agreement.   The place appointed for the conference
was some distance from the fort, and thither Zebulon
proceeded, taking with him, as a precaution, 400 men
well armed, comprising the main strength of the garrison.   Not a living creature was found on the spot agreed
on, and Zebulon, anxious for an interview, advanced
farther from the fort toward the foot of the mountain.
As he proceeded onward the solitude grew more dismal
and the absence of human beings more remarkable.
But as if urged onward by an irresistible destiny, he
still continued his forward march.   The country began
to be overshaded by the dense forests, and the tall oaks
to twine their branches high in air across the path ;
but fate still impelled him to go on.   Just then a flag
was discovered in the path some distance ahead that
seemed to wave him on.   The individual who bore it
appeared as if afraid of treachery from his side, and
retired as he advanced, still making the same signals.
He pressed forward still faster in order to assure the
traitors that he would not betray them.   But the
unfortunate Americans had been already betrayed
instead.   Taking advantage of the dense thickets,
Brandt's forces had completely surrounded them, and

their fancied dream of security was suddenly broken in
upon by the terrible war-whoop as hundreds of savages
sprang from their ambush, and with hideous yells
attacked the devoted band from every side. In the
midst of the confusion that ensued, Zebulon displayed
more courage than would have been thought possible
considering the simplicity of his previous proceedings.
He formed his men into a hollow square, and the fierce
onset of the savages was met with such a determined
volley, as to at once check them. Though surprised,
the Americans acted with such vigor and resolution
that they quickly had the advantage on their side ; but
just then a soldier, either through cowardice or treachery, cried out. "The Colonel has ordered a retreat."
The soldiers at once gave way, and the Indians with
terrible yells leaped in among the ranks. A horrible
carnage ensued. Those who ran, fell by the pursuing
bullet—those who resisted, by the knife, club, or tomahawk. The dead, dying, wounded and struggling,
friends and foes—were heaped together promiscuously,
while from the mass arose shrieks of agony and yells of
victory, supplications for mercy and threats of vengeance
such as had never before been dreamed of in that
hitherto happy valley. Happy were those who died
the soonest! The savages reserved their captives for
more cruel tortures, while the Tories, more bloodthirsty
still, actually tore the faces of the prisoners with their
finger-nails. Never was rout so deplorable. Only
about sixty of the four hundred escaped the butchery,
and these, with Zebulon, made their way to a redout on
the other bank of the Susquehanna.

The victors immediately invested Fort Kingston anew,
and to terrify the remainder of the garrison they hurled
over the walls about two hundred scalps still dripping

with the blood of their murdered brethren. Seeing the impossibility of defense, Col. Dennison, who commanded the fort, sent a flag to John Butler to inquire what terms would be allowed the garrison if they should surrender the fort. He returned as an answer— " The hatchet!" In this dreadful extremity, the Colonel made what resistance he could, and fought bravely till his soldiers were nearly all killed, when he was forced to surrender at discretion. The savages entered the fort and began to drag out the vanquished, who, knowing what hands they were in, expected no mercy, found none, and met their fate without a cry. Becoming tired of killing in detail, the savages bethought themselves of a new expedient. They enclosed the men, women and children in the houses and barracks, set them on fire, and consumed all within—listening with delight to the moans and shrieks, and dancing with hellish glee at the occasional glimpses they caught of the death struggles of the expiring multitude.

One more fort, that of Wilkesbarre, still remained in the hands of the colonists of Wyoming. This the victors next presented themselves before and demanded its surrender. Those within, hoping to find mercy if they made no resistance, surrendered at discretion. But if opposition exasperated these insatiable tigers for human blood, submission did not soften them. The soldiers of the garrison were first put to death by means of tortures such as only barbarity could devise. Then the men, women, and children were shut up in the houses as before, fire was applied, and that unfeeling element soon stilled their cries with death, and left nought but ashes to mark their mortal remains.

Capt. Bedlock, of Fort Wilkesbarre, was stripped naked and his body stuck full of sharp pine splinters; a heap of the same material was then piled around him and set on fire. His two associates, Captains Ransom and Durgee, were then thrown alive into the flames, and all perished together.

One Tory, whose mother had married a second husband, butchered her with his own hand, and afterwards massacred his father-in-law, his sisters, and their infants in the cradle. Another killed his father and exterminated all his family. A third imbrued his hands in the blood of his brothers, his sisters, his brother-in-law and his father-in-law. "These," says Eastman, "were a part only of the horrors perpetrated by the loyalists and Indians at the excision of Wyoming. Other atrocities, if possible still more abominable, we leave in silence."

The forts being in their hands, they next proceeded to the devastation of the country. In doing this they called into requisition at once fire, sword, and all instruments of destruction. The crops of every description were consigned to the flames. Habitations, granaries, and buildings, the fruits of years of toil and industry, sank into barren ruins in the track of these fell demons. "But," says Eastman, "who will believe that their fury, not yet satiated upon human creatures, was also wreaked upon the very beasts? That they cut out the tongues of horses and cattle, and left them to wander in the midst of those fields, lately so luxuriant, and now in desolation, seeming to enjoy the torments of their lingering death?"

Many women and children had escaped while the foe was busy dispatching their husbands and fathers. These were no less worthy of commiseration than those who had died. Dispersed and wandering in the forests as chance or fear directed their footsteps, without food,

without clothes, without guide, these defenseless fugitives suffered every degree of distress. The most
robust and resolute alone escaped ; the others perished,
and their bodies, with those of their hapless infants,
became the prey of wild beasts.

The father of the late Dr. Merit H. Cash, of Wawayanda, was among those who escaped this massacre. He
was at that time a very small boy, and his mother led
him by the hand through the wilderness for days, sub-
sisting entirely upon the berries, &c., which they found
on their way, till they were at last fortunate enough to
reach the Minisink settlement.

Benjamin Whittaker, with his daughter, also escaped.
They had removed to Wyoming but about three years
before, having previously resided on the farm now
owned by Mr. William H. Mead, near Brookfield, in the
present town of Wawayanda. They were in the fort at
Wyoming when it surrendered, and were both saved.
Brandt took her by the hair of the head with one hand
and painted her face with red paint with the other,
telling her that that was the mark of safety. She afterwards married William Fullerton, Jr., whose descendants were formerly large property owners in Wawayanda, and are generally known throughout Orange
county. (Eager's History, p. 414.)

At the capture of the same fort, when the Indians
came flocking in, the settlers threw down their arms,
and with the women and children huddled in one corner
expecting instant death. A little lad named John
Finch, amused at the odd appearance of the Indians,
laughed at them. One of them raised his tomahawk to
strike him down, but Brandt interfered and ordered
him to let the boy go. He afterwards found his way
to Minisink. Many of his relatives for a long time

resided in the town of Mount Hope, and the village of Finchville is named after them.

A lady named Christina Wood was in one of the forts of Wyoming with her husband and family. Her husband and son were killed, and she was approached by an Indian with an uplifted tomahawk. She had an infant in her arms, and when the little innocent saw the savage approach it looked up into his face and smiled. The savage made a motion as if to make the child the first victim, seeing which the mother held it closer to her bosom. He gazed upon them for a moment, but the smile of innocence had touched his heart—the tomahawk fell by his side harmless, and he walked away and left them. She escaped, and found her way to Goshen with her child, where she afterwards died at the age of eighty-five. A survivor of the massacre, Asa A. Gore, died at Preston, Connecticut, January, 1850, aged eighty-one years and five months. His mother was one of those who escaped, and she carried him in her arms through the woods to Minisink.

Mrs. John Weeden, supposed to be the last survivor of the massacre, died in Columbia, Lorain county, Ohio, on Friday, April 13th, 1860, aged ninety-three years. Her maiden name was Martin. She and her father, mother and sister, escaped, and with a flag of truce traveled through the forest to within forty miles of the Connecticut river, where her older brother met them and then took them to Colchester. She was twelve years old at the time; was born in 1766, and married in 1798.

CHAPTER VIII.

On the 13th of October (1778) succeeding the Wyoming Massacre, a band of about one hundred Indians
and Tories, under command of Brandt, invaded the
upper, or Peenpack, neighborhood. It is needless to
say that their appearance was the signal for a general
panic, so fearful had been their atrocities at Wyoming
and Cherry Valley, which latter place had been deso-
lated by them shortly after the former. They surprised
the family of a Mr. Westfall, among the first of their
acts in Peenpack, and killed the only man that was at
home at the time. Mr. Thomas Swartout and his four
sons, thinking that perhaps the invaders were few in
number, and more intent on plunder than actual war,
resolved to defend their own house. The women were
sent to the fort at Gumaer's, and the house firmly barri-
caded. But when the enemy appeared, their number
at once convinced the little band of Spartans of the
futility of defense. They fired a few times at the foe,
but seeing their chances of retreat would soon be cut
off, they resolved to endeavor to escape. Accordingly
they all started and ran in the direction of the fort; but
a bullet pierced the skull of one of the young men before
they reached the shelter of the barn. One of the sons

separated from the others and ran toward the Never-sink river, a half mile off. He was pursued by a detachment of the Indians, and shot while swimming the river, near the opposite shore. The old man and his two other sons kept together, and ran on as fast as they were able toward the fort. It soon became appar-ent to them that their efforts would be all in vain, as they were destined to be overtaken. The old man paused. "James," said he to one of his sons, "you are young and active and can save yourself. If you stay to assist me we shall all be killed. Save yourself while you can!" The young man took his father's advice, and started on with increased speed. The other son kept by the side of his father, and both were soon overtaken and tomahawked. James was closely pursued for over half a mile through brush and briers, over fences and across lots, till he at last reached the fort at Gumaer's, and the enemy had to abandon the chase.

The continued firing warned the inhabitants of the country of the approaching danger, and they at once repaired to the forts at Gumaer's and De Witt's, aban-doning that at Du Puy's, as they had no troops to garrison it. The fort at Gumaer's had only nine regu-lars to defend it, and was but a small picket fort at best. Capt. Cuddeback, who commanded it, was aware of the influence display oftentimes made on the Indian mind, and he resolved to profit by it. He ordered all the men and women, both young and old, to the rear of the fort. Next he had all the spare guns and sticks that could be found, together with all the old hats, coats and breeches, brought forward. The guns and sticks were placed in the hands of those who were unarmed, and the old clothes were used to change the appearance of the women. Many a blushing damsel, who two days before

would have scorned the idea of her ever wearing male
attire, made her appearance that day in a cocked hat
and ragged coat and vest, with her dainty limbs clad in
a faded pair of homespun breeches ; and many a staid
matron was that day apparently transformed into a
dignified Continental soldier, with a blue coat and brass
buttons. When the enemy came in sight the Captain
ordered the drums to beat, and placing himself at the
head of his forces, marched them in Indian file around
to the front of the fort and entered it, giving the
Indians a distant, distinct, and consequently enlarged
view of the garrison. This done, the women and
children were ordered into the cellar as they could be
of no further use ; but an elderly lady, Anna Swartout,
the widow of James Swartout, Sr., refused to go, telling
the Captain that she would take a pitchfork with which
she had just marched in the fort, and remain with the
men. Her request was granted, and she walked about
with the fork in true military bearing, anxiously watching the movements of the enemy, and ready to give
them a taste of woman's courage should any ·of them
attempt to enter. The Indians halted before coming
within gunshot. The fort was situated on an open
plain, and they knew the settlers to be good marksmen.
Besides, they evidently supposed the garrison to have
been reinforced, from the number of soldiers they had
seen. After a few shots were exchanged without effect
upon either side, they passed by, and the fort was
saved by Capt. Cuddeback's strategem.

Brandt's forces then proceeded to Fort DeWitt.
Here they stationed themselves on a hill which was
covered with woods near the fort, and remained some
time, firing occasionally as they obtained a view of the
garrison, but without effect, if we except the killing of

Captain Newkirk's horse by a stray bullet. They then retreated toward the west the same day, after having burned all the houses, barns, &c., they found in their course; a circumstance that afterwards distressed the inhabitants much for the want of hay, grain and articles of furniture. And thus ended Brandt's first invasion of the Minisink Region. DuPuy and one or two others had sent their wives and children to Major Phillips', at Phillipsburg, (a small village in the eastern part of what is now the town of Wawayanda,) for safety. The danger of the Minisink people thus became known, and Major Phillips arrived at Fort Gumaer the day after the invasion, with a company of militia. But the spoilers had departed, and pursuit was useless. Several women and children were sent for protection to Mr. James Finch's, where Finchville now stands, in the south-western part of the town of Mount Hope.

This invasion thoroughly aroused the inhabitants to a sense of their exposed situation, and the members of the committee of safety immediately took steps to increase the defensive powers of the settlement. The forts were repaired as well as the limited number of the garrison would permit, and an application was at once made to the general government for help. Their petition was acted upon without delay, and the brave Count Pulaski, with a battalion of cavalry, sent to their assistance. The presence of these veterans inspired the settlers with new courage. Many of them brought their families back and proceeded to refit their homes and recommence clearing their lands. The winter glided away without any signs of the savage foe, and they began to hope that their share of the turmoils of war was at an end.

In February, (1779,) deeming their presence no longer

necessary, Count Pulaski and his men were ordered to
South Carolina. They left their winter quarters with
regret; for their stay, though short, had been a pleasant
one. The inhabitants too regretted the parting, for besides the respect they felt for Pulaski and his troops,
they foresaw themselves left in a defenseless condition.
Some time however elapsed after the departure, and they
were not disturbed. The spring almost imperceptibly
melted into summer. The birds returned from their
southern homes, and again cheered the laborers by the
noisy Neversink and sparkling Delaware with their
songs. Prosperity reigned supreme, and Minisink
seemed destined after all for a favored region. But
alas ! it was only the calm that precedes the storm. Even
as we have sometimes seen a cloudless summer day terminate in a mingled tornado of wind, lightning and rain
—just so was the serenity of the settlement of Minisink
broken, on the 20th of July, 1779, by Brandt and his
band of Tories and Indians. Just before daylight on
that morning they surprised the fort at Major Decker's.
The men had departed for their work pretty early, and
the only occupants of the house were two negro boys;
the women having gone the day before to Fort Gumaer.
The negroes were made prisoners, and the Indians then
searched the premises for plunder. Some liquor was
found, and the party was disposed to make a carousal
of it; but Brandt quickly stopped it by destroying the
liquor. A tavern had been kept for years before the
war at this place. Fire was then applied to the buildings, and the invaders departed for the dwelling of
Anthony Van Etten.

James Swartout, who escaped so narrowly from the
Indians in the first invasion, had just entered a black-
smith shop kept by a negro at Mr. Van Etten's, when

he saw the Indians coming. No other place for secretion presenting itself, he crept up the chimney. The negro remained in the shop, knowing the Indians seldom injured a person of color. The Indians entered, and seeing no one but the negro, began throwing the tools around as if for sport. One of them took hold of the handle of the bellows and began to blow the fire furiously. The negro, knowing the effect that the heat and smoke would have on his friend in the chimney, told the Indian he would spoil that thing if he did not stop. He good naturedly ceased, and soon after with his companions left the shop. Swartout came down almost choked with smoke and dust, and nearly exhausted with the effort needed to keep his position for so long a time. (Eager's History, p. 338.) While the enemy was busy burning Van Etten's buildings, he escaped.

One detachment of Indians went to the house of Jas. Van Vliet. The inmates discovered them approaching and fled. A man named Roolif Cuddeback was there at the time, and ran toward the woods in a different direction from the others. The foremost Indian, some distance in advance of his companions, at once started in pursuit. Cuddeback, finding that he would be overtaken, and that but one Indian was following him, suddenly turned and faced him. The Indian threw his tomahawk at him, but it struck a bush and he dodged it. They then grasped in a hand-to-hand struggle—both unarmed except a knife which the Indian had in his belt. For this fatal instrument they both struggled. At last it fell to the ground, and neither could stoop to pick it up with safety. The contest lasted till both were nearly exhausted. Cuddeback afterwards said that he was more than a match for the Indian, but the

latter became naked, and his skin was so slippery with
grease and sweat that he could get no hold of him.
Finally the Indian broke away from him, and ran off in
the woods.   It was reported afterwards that the Indian
died in a few years of injuries received in this encounter.
The father of this Indian was shot while crossing the
river on horseback, by Capt. Cuddeback, a brother of
James.   (Eager's History, p. 389.)

Another party of the Indians set fire to a number of
buildings near Carpenter's Point; among others, to the
old Machackemeck church.   Many of the inhabitants on
this morning had gone to attend a funeral.   The first
intimation of danger they had was an alarm of "Indians;" and on rushing to the open air the smoke and
flames of burning houses were seen rising among the
trees in every direction.   The very name of Brandt
caused many a cheek to blanch with fear.   Some of the
assemblage at once started for the settlements on the
east side of the Shawangunk mountain.   The others fled
to the different forts.   The Indians met Major Decker,
who was on horseback.   They shot at, and wounded
him, but he put spurs to his horse and escaped.

At the Van Auken fort, the Indians fired a volley,
killing one of the garrison.   An Indian then undertook
to creep up to one of the buildings to set it on fire, but
was detected in the act and shot.

At the same time a party of Indians, says Eager, visited the school house, and threatened to exterminate
one generation of the settlement at a blow.   Here an
incident took place, proving that the great Indian leader
was possessed of human feelings, despite his ferocity.
The teacher, Jeremiah Van Auken, was led about a half
a mile from the school house and killed.   Some of the
boys were slain by the tomahawk, and the rest fled to

the woods; while the little girls, bewildered with horror, gathered around the dead body of their teacher and gazed in speechless fright at the terrible scene. A moment more and the attention of the savages would be directed from the boys to them. In this dread emergency, a tall, powerful Indian came along, and with a brush hurriedly dashed some black paint on their aprons, telling them to " Hold up the mark when they saw an Indian coming, and it would save them;" then with a yell or warwhoop he disappeared in the woods. The tall Indian was none other than Brandt, and the children were safe. When the girls saw the Indians coming they held up their aprons with the black mark, and were not disturbed. An idea suggested itself to them, and with woman's wit they quickly adopted it. The boys were called from their hiding places, and the girls pressed the black mark upon their outer garments. It left a distinct impression, and this the boys held to view when the Indians passed, with a like happy effect.

Mrs. Sarah Van Auken did not succeed in getting within the protection of the fort, and saved her life by creeping into an old ditch. (Eager's History, p. 390.)

During this incursion the Indians and Tories burned everything that came in their way—houses, barns, granaries and goods—in short, all that the flames could destroy. Those of the inhabitants who could not get to the forts in time to escape the fury of the savages, fled through the forest to Goshen, and the settlements east of the Shawangunk.

Benjamin Whittaker and family, who after their escape from the Wyoming Massacre, had settled on the Delaware, were again forced to flee for safety. His daughter Mary, according to Eager, hid herself among the straw in an old potato hole and thus escaped, though

5

the Indians came searching for her, and stood on the
boards, so near her that she could have touched their
feet with her hands.

Major Decker's wife escaped through the woods to
. Mr. James Finch's, the present site of Finchville, where
she came leading her small children by the hand, with
hardly clothes enough to cover their backs, and weeping
piteously. The only article she saved of her household
goods was a small bible which she carried under her
arm.

The enemy after completing the work of destruction
and plunder fell back slowly on their line of retreat.
They were confident that in point of numbers the settlers could not bring a force to compete with them
under a week or ten days; their own force numbering,
according to Dr. Wilson, three hundred Indian warriors
and two hundred Tories painted to resemble Indians.
Other accounts place their numbers at one hundred and
eighty, and one or two as low as one hundred and sixty.
Be this as it may, they were sufficiently confident to
proceed leisurley on their return, and on the evening of
the 21st encamped at Half-way Brook.

CHAPTER IX.

Intelligence of the ravages of Brandt's band of savages was brought to Goshen on the evening of the 20th, the same day of their invasion. The public mind was greatly excited by the tidings. At the reports of their barbarous murders, which were doubtless much exaggerated by the panic stricken fugitives, work of all kinds was abandoned and the men gathered together in groups, each proposing plans for punishing the enemy, which were as absurd as impracticable. The children left their play and listened eagerly to the fearful tales told by older persons of the doings of the foe, while many a matron's face blanched with terror at the name of Brandt, whose ferocities at Wyoming and Cherry Valley were still fresh in their memory. One man amidst the confusion acted with promptness and decision. This was Col. Benjamin Tusten, commander of the local militia in the Goshen neighborhood. He at once dispatched messengers to the officers of his regiment, with orders to rendezvous at the "lower neighborhood" in Minisink the next morning, with as many volunteers as they could raise. Word was also sent to Col. Hathorn, commander of the Warwick regiment of militia, to meet him at the same place. We may well suppose that many a volunteer passed a

sleepless night in common with the affrighted families
of Goshen, on that momentous night of the 20th of
July, 1779. The dawn of the next morning witnessed
the departure of many of the bravest citizens east of
the Shawangunk mountain, numbers of them heads of
families, eager to revenge the massacre of their friends
by coping with the dreaded foe, but little aware that
the direful visions of disaster and woe that had flitted
before their wakeful eyes during the long hours of the
previous night were soon to be realized ; little aware
that the tearful "good-bye" of the dear ones at home,
was a farewell that would last till they met beyond the
veil that conceals the confines of eternity from our view.

> "Ah! then and there was hurrying to and fro,
>   And gathering tears, and tremblings of distress,
> And cheeks all pale, which but an hour ago
>   Blush'd at the praise of their own loveliness ;
> And there were sudden partings, such as press
>   The life from out young hearts, and choking sighs
> Which ne'er might be repeated—who could guess
>   If ever more should meet, those mutual eyes,
> Since upon night so sweet, such awful morn could rise."

At a seasonable hour that morning, one hundred and
forty-nine men assembled at Minisink and placed themselves under command of Col. Tusten. A council was
immediately held to decide upon a plan of action. The
majority were in favor of instant pursuit. But here the
good sense of Col. Tusten interposed for the success of
his little army. He reminded them that the enemy far
outnumbered them, was accompanied by Tories who
were better acquainted with the ground than they, and
commanded by Col. Brandt, whose previous expeditions
had proved his cunning and generalship—while they
lacked ammunition, and were few in number compared
with the foe. He proposed that they should wait where

they were for reinforcements and ammuniton which would be with them in a short time. The majority were deaf to these proposals. They affected to consider the Indians cowardly, and were for pursuing them at once and retaking their plunder. In the midst of the debate, one Major Meeker mounted his horse, and flourishing his sword with a braggadocio air, cried out, "Let the brave men follow me ; the cowards may stay behind." The effect may well be imagined, for this is not the only instance where bravado has drowned the voice of judgment and sense. The question was decided, and the entire party took its line of march over the old Kathleghton path, the trail of the retreating savages. Seventeen miles was accomplished the same afternoon, and the pursuers then encamped for the night at a place known as Skinner's Saw Mills. The next morning (the 22d) they were joined by Col. Hathorn of the Warwick regiment, with a small reinforcement. The command was then taken by Col. Hathorn, he being an older officer than Col. Tusten. They then marched a few miles to Half-way Brook, and there came across the place where the Indians had encamped the preceding night. Another council was then held, and though Col. Tusten proved to them that they were outnumbered, by the number and extent of the camp fires that had dotted the enemy's camping ground, the same bravado that had ruled the day previous gained the decision, and the line of march was again taken up. Col. Tyler, who was best informed of the forest, was sent ahead with a small scouting party, as it was evident the foe was but a short distance in advance. He had gone but a little way however, before he fell into an ambuscade and was killed. This timely warning, says Dawson, fell unnoticed upon the reckless mass that followed.

After the alarm had subsided, the advice of their abler officers was again disregarded, and the settlers madly rushed forward.

About nine o'clock in the morning as they were marching over the high hills east of the Delaware, they spied the Indians about three-quarters of a mile ahead, leisurely proceeding along the bank of the river toward the fording place at the mouth of the Lackawaxen. Col. Hathorn, supposing his troops had been unnoticed by the enemy, and wishing to intercept them before they reached the ford, moved off the trail toward the right and soon lost sight of them, owing to the intervening hills. Brandt had observed the Americans and anticipated their movement. As soon as they disappeared he at once wheeled his columns to the right, and passed up a deep ravine directly in the rear of the pursuers, thus choosing his own ground for the coming battle. By this maneuver about fifty of Hathorn's men became separated from the main body, and were not in the engagement. The Americans reached the fording place about ten o'clock, and discovered some of Brandt's men crossing the Delaware with the plunder. One Indian was behind the others, riding a horse which was recognized by the settlers as having been stolen from Minisink the day before. He was pursued to the river and shot while crossing. (Stone's Life of Brandt.) At the same instant another Indian appeared directly on the path over which they had just passed, while to add to the surprise of the Americans it was found that Brandt was not on the path he had been following when last seen. Brandt afterwards said that he arose from his hiding place at this juncture and addressed the officer in command of the settlers, demanding their surrender, and telling them his force far outnumbered theirs; but while engaged in parleying, a ball from their ranks passed through his belt, and he then retired to his men. About eleven o'clock the action became general. The settlers found themselves in a complete ambuscade. Every rock, tree and bush that surrounded them, seemed to furnish shelter for an enemy. Only about ninety in number, they found themselves almost overwhelmed, but forming into a hollow square on the summit of a small hill, occupying about an acre, they hid behind trees and rocks, and "fought like brave men long and well." Suddenly the voice of Brandt was heard above the shouts and yells and roar of musketry, commanding the Indians who had crossed the Delaware with the plunder, to return. It was said that those who survived the battle never forgot the trumpet-tones of that deep, powerful voice. The Indians at once obeyed their chief, and crossing the river, fell with fury upon the rear of the Americans, who now beheld themselves completely surrounded. Their access to water being cut off, thirst was added to their torments. To increase their dismay, their ammunition began to be exhausted, and the sun was rapidly going down in the west, betokening the close of the day.

The day had passed, how they hardly knew. Repeated attempts of the enemy to break their lines had failed, for they were good marksmen, and Col. Hathorn had ordered them not to fire a single shot till the enemy were near enough to make their aim sure. Just as the sun sank behind the western hills, a man who had guarded the north-east angle of the square, and whose trusty rifle had carried death to the foe more than once during the day, incautiously exposed himself to view while shifting his position behind a rock which sheltered him. A half-dozen or more Indian rifles cracked in

unison, and the brave man fell back dead. Brandt's
quick eye saw the opening, and followed by his troops
he dashed like a resistless deluge into the very midst
of the Americans. They ceased to resist and fled in all
directions. Some swam the Delaware, and many were
drowned while attempting to cross. A horrible massacre ensued, and more were killed in the pursuit than in
the battle. The yells of the savages, the cries for
mercy, the groans of the dying, and the heart-rending
supplications of the wounded for their companions not
to forsake them, presented a scene that baffles description. Col. Tusten, who was a skillful surgeon, was
engaged in dressing the wounds of the wounded, seventeen of whom were under his care behind a cliff of rocks.
He remained with them, and died the death of a brave
man, while those who had so freely called him a coward
previously, were ingloriously running for their lives.
Had the fifty men who were cut off from the main body,
done their duty by attacking the enemy in the rear,
instead of lying in a swamp all day like a parcel of
frightened women, the fortunes of the day might have
been turned against the foe and many lives saved. Of
those actually engaged in the battle, forty-four were
killed, according to Dr. Wilson's account, while Dawson
says that of the one hundred and forty-nine men who
went out, only thirty returned.

NAMES OF THE KILLED AS FAR AS KNOWN.

Col. Benjamin Tusten,	Robert Townsend,
Capt. Bezaliel Tyler,	Samuel Knapp,
Capt. Benjamin Vail,	James Knapp,
Capt. John Duncan,	Benjamin Bennett,
Capt. Samuel Jones,	William Barker,
Capt. John Little,	Jacob Dunning,

Lieut. John Wood,
Adj. Nathaniel Fitch,
Ens. Ephraim Masten,
Ens. Ephraim Middaugh,
Gabriel Wisner,
Stephen Mead,
Nathaniel Terwilliger,
Joshua Lockwood,
Ephraim Ferguson,
—— Talmadge,
John Carpenter,
David Barney,
Gamaliel Bailey,
Moses Thomas,
Jonathan Haskell,
Abram Williams,
Daniel Reed,

Jonathan Pierce,
James Little,
Joseph Norris,
Gilbert S. Vail,
· Joel Decker,
Abram Shepherd,
—— Shepherd,
Nathan Wade,
Simon Wait,
James Mosher,
Isaac Ward,
Baltus Niepos,
Eleazer Owens,
Adam Embler,
Samuel Little,
Benjamin Dunning.

The Moses Thomas who was killed, was a son of Moses Thomas, Sr., one of the first settlers at Cochecton, and who was killed in an Indian attack on that place in 1763. He enlisted early in the war, and was with the army at West Point and Newburgh; but becoming dissatisfied with his officers he hired a substitute and returned to his family in Minisink. When Brandt invaded that section, he was among the first to volunteer in pursuit, and was slain in the battle by a Tory named Case Cole. (Quinlan's Life of Tom Quick, p. 174.)

John Howel, the ancestor of an old family of Wawayanda, Orange county, was in this battle, and when the Americans broke and fled, stepped behind a tree and pulled off his shoes. Just then a tall Indian came along and stopped close by him, resting the butt of his gun on the ground and gazing after the fugitives, glimpses

5*

of whom could frequently be seen among the brush on the hill sides. Mr. Howel saw that the Indian would soon become aware of his presence, and determined to be beforehand with him ; so he took good aim at his head and fired. He said he never knew whether he killed the Indian or not, for he ran as fast as possible and did not look back to see. He was not pursued however, and escaped.

Major Wood had heard that Brandt was a Freemason, and having by some process become acquainted with the Master Mason's signal of distress, when overtaken by the Indians and about to be dispatched, he gave the signal. Faithful to his pledge, Brandt interposed and saved his life. When he found out his mistake afterwards, he was very angry, but nevertheless spared his life. Eager says that the evening after the battle, when the Indians were about to tie him, Wood remonstrated, said he was a gentleman, and promised not to escape. Brandt acceeded to his request, but directed him to lie on a blanket between two Indians; who were directed to tomahawk him if he tried to escape during the night. The blanket caught fire in the night, but he dared not stir or make a noise for fear he should experience the reality of the threat, and be tomahawked. The fire at last reached his feet and he kicked it out. The blanket belonged to Brandt, and he treated Wood harshly ever after. When asked the reason he replied, " D—n you, you burnt my blanket!" Wood ultimately returned to his friends after a long captivity.

James Reeve, grandfather of John H. Reeve and James M. Reeve, Esqs., of Wawayanda, was in the battle. When the settlers gave way he fled with the rest, but after crossing the Delaware separated from his companions. While making his way through the woods his arm became weary with carrying his gun so long in one hand, and he thought he would carry it with the other awhile. When he made the exchange the gun fell from his hand, and on investigating the matter, he was surprised to find his arm had been broken by a musket ball; his mind having been so occupied that he had not felt the pain.

A man named Cuddeback was among the fugitives, and fled with his companions till he became completely exhausted. He then stepped from the path and hid among some small bushes. After a short time the Indians came along in pursuit and happily passed without seeing him. He was just about rising to his feet in order to get farther in the woods, when he saw an Indian coming. The Indian discovered him when about opposite ; but Cuddeback had his rifle ready, and the moment he saw the Indian's eye rest on him, he fired. He then fled with all possible speed, not knowing whether he had hit the Indian. No one pursued him however, and he escaped.

Col. Benjamin Tusten, who was killed, was a practising physician of the town of Goshen. His father removed from Southhold, Long Island, in the year 1746, and settled on the patent granted to Mrs. Denn, the first settler on the Wawayanda patent, which was between two and three miles from the village of Goshen, on the banks of the Otterkill. The old gentleman was much respected, and was a judge for some time in the county court. He was afterward appointed colonel of the militia. He owned a large tract of land, and intended young Benjamin for a farmer; he being three years of age at the time of removal. But as he grew older he evinced a great desire to adopt some professional calling. For this purpose he attended several medical schools, and in 1769 commenced the practice of physic at his father's house. In 1770 he introduced inoculation as a preventive of the small pox; the first of its general trial in Orange county. At the age of twenty-eight he married a Miss Brown, whom he had become acquainted with while studying medicine with Dr. Burnet, at Newark, N. J. When the Revolution commenced he took an active part against the arbitrary measures of England. He was appointed Lieutenant-Colonel of the Goshen regiment of militia, under Gen. Allison, in 1777, and the following year Surrogate of Orange county, which office he held when killed at Minisink. (Eager's History.)

Daniel Myers, an early settler of the present town of Minisink, and much noted for his hatred of the Indians, was in this battle. When the whites gave way, he thought he would wait till the first rush was over in hopes of a better chance to escape. Accordingly he stepped out of sight behind a large tree. After waiting some time he concluded the Indians had gone away after those who had run, and ventured to look out from his place of concealment. As he did so, an Indian who had remained behind for some purpose, spied him, and dodged behind a tree with a yell. They were within close gunshot of each other, and at once began maneuvering to get the first shot. They were both good marksmen, and they each knew that if the other had a chance to aim at a vital part his life would pay the forfeit. At last Myers bethought him of an expedient. He drew the ramrod from his rifle and hung his hat upon it. He then pushed the hat around the side of the tree very cautiously, as if it were himself trying to get a glimpse of his opponent. The ruse was successful. The Indian fired, with such an accurate aim as to send a bullet plumb through the centre of the hat. Myers let the hat fall; and the Indian thinking he had killed him, sprang forward with a whoop of triumph to secure his scalp. Myers then stepped in view, and as the Indian paused with astonishment, shot him through the heart. Descendants of this brave old pioneer, or of his relatives, still reside in the towns of Minisink and Greenville.

Benjamin Dunning, at the close of the battle, tried to escape by crossing the Delaware with a number of others. The Indians kept up a terrible fire on those in the water, and several were killed. He escaped unhurt till just as he was climbing from the water on the opposite side, when a bullet struck him and he fell dead upon the bank. His uncle, Daniel Dunning, formerly resided near Ridgebury in the town of Wawayanda.

Of Major Meeker, who acted so prominent a part in the movements of the troops preceding the battle of Minisink, a humorous incident has been preserved to us by tradition, illustrative of the influence of the price of an article regardless of its quality. Shortly after he became chosen to the rank of Major of the militia, he found it necessary to procure corresponding equipments, and for this purpose visited Newburgh. Chief among the military toggery desired, was a hat—an article, the flaunt of whose proud feather, and the glitter of the shield that fastened its turned up side, had long visited the dreams of the ambitious Major. It had been decided on as one that should only be equaled by the best dressed officer of the brigade; and with this thought uppermost he entered the chief hat store of the place. He was shown one, with the style and fit of which he expressed himself pleased, and was told the price was only five dollars. " But," said the Major, " isn't that rather low? To be sure it is very nice, and no doubt

good, but have you no higher priced ones ?" " Certainly," replied the hatter, and taking the hat he passed
into a back room apparently to change it. Here he
turned the feather a little more to the other side,
brushed it thoroughly and in a few minutes brought out
the same one. " That's a beauty," exclaimed the de-
lighted Major; " What is the price of it ?" " Ten dollars," was the reply. " I'll take that one," said the
Major, and paying the money he walked away much
better suited at having paid ten dollars for the military
covering of his caput instead of five.

There is an old tradition current among the legends
of Minisink and Greenville, that Joseph Brandt in order
to acquaint himself with the state of affairs in the Minisink neighborhood, paid it a visit in secret, some time
before his second invasion, and remained concealed in a
swamp in the present town of Greenville, nearly a
month. The neighbors suspected a certain man, who
had expressed Tory sentiments pretty freely, of carrying victuals to the swamp for some purpose, supposing
probably it was some stray Indian secreted there.
They set a watch upon the Tory, and one morning
caught him just before daylight returning from the
swamp, whither he had been to carry the carcass of a
sheep he had just slaughtered. A council of the citizens
was called, and many plans suggested for his punish-
ment, as he refused to tell whom he had been feeding.
It was at last determined to drive him to Goshen on
foot. The skin of the sheep he had killed was thoroughly
wound about him, a soldier followed with his bayonet
fixed to keep him from lagging, a boy brought up the
rear with an old bass drum, and in this order he was
marched to Goshen to jail, a distance of some sixteen
miles; a feat that must have made him look somewhat

sheepish, as it was a broiling hot day in summer. We may well be assured too, that the settlers in Greenville felt somewhat sheepish when they found out what an important personage had been concealed beneath their very noses, and allowed to escape with impunity, when a very little energy would have captured him.

Brandt by the above means became well informed of the nature and resources of the neighborhood, and thus was enabled to invade the Minisink Region so successfully. The same knowledge enabled him so skilfully to defeat the irregular levies that pursued him, whose hasty action and ill-advised movements he naturally understood from their ignorance of war, and was well prepared to take advantage of. A few days after this battle he fell with the same suddenness upon a settlement in the valley of the Mohawk, and left it a smoking ruin. His success rendered his name a potent spell of fear, far and near. He was generally believed to have been a half-breed—his mother a Mohawk squaw and his father a German—but it has since been thought he was a pure Mohawk Indian. He acquired a good education at Dartmouth College, and was appointed to a Colonel's commission of the Six Nations, under George III. at the commencement of the Revolution. Education did not tame his savage nature, for says Dr. Wilson, "In him the blood of the barbarian extinguished every spark of civilization that might have been kindled in his constitution. He was more cunning than the fox, and fiercer than the tiger." Immediate movements were made by the government to check these depredations upon the frontier settlements. General Sullivan, with three thousand men, ascended the Susquehanna to Tioga Point, near the present village of Waverly, where he was met by Gen. Clinton, who with one thousand, had marched from the Mohawk by the way of Cherry Valley. Uniting their forces they proceeded against the Senecas, whose principal stations were on the banks of the Genesee. The Indians hearing of the projected expedition, took possession of an elevated piece of ground near Newton, on the Tioga river, and fortified it with judgment. Here the combined forces of Sullivan and Clinton attacked them in August, the month after the Minisink battle. For two hours they stood a fierce cannonading, but at length their trenches were forced and they fled precipitately. The victorious army penetrated into the very heart of their country, and laid it desolate. Their villages, with their detached habitations, their immense crops of growing corn and grain, fruit trees, and gardens, were indiscriminately destroyed. So heavy did the hand of retribution fall upon them, that though they occasionally made feeble irruptions into small settlements along the Mohawk, they never after were able to muster force enough to advance so far east as Minisink.

For forty-three years the bones of the victims of the Minisink battle were bleached and whitened by the sun, wind and rain, among the dark ravines and on the bleak hillside where they fell. They were not forgotten, for the fearful scenes attending the death struggle, and the cause in which they bravely fought and died, had stamped its impress indelibly upon the memory of their fellow citizens. The first attempt to recover their remains was made by the widows of the killed, of whom there were thirty-three in the Presbyterian congregation of Goshen. They undertook to proceed to the battle field on horseback, but had not gone far before they were forced to give up the task. The man they hired to guide them to the place, was paid liberally and promised to go

on and secure the remains.   But he proved faithless to
his trust, and was never heard from afterward.   In 1820
Dr. David R. Arnell published a sketch of Col. Tusten
who was killed at the battle.   It awoke a new interest
in the matter, and finally led to the appointment of a
committee to gather up the bones.   The committee
passed the night at the house of Mr. Samuel Watkins, of
Half-way Brook, a descendant of Samuel Watkins of
Revolutionary fame; having traveled about forty miles
the first day.   The next day they proceeded to the
battle field.   This is in the town of Lumberland, Sullivan county, opposite the mouth of the Lackawaxen.   It
commenced on the banks of the Delaware and ended
about three-fourths of a mile from the river.   Some of
the bones were found several miles distant, in the
woods, the whole vicinity being a dense wilderness.
Some have thought that Indian bones were picked up
with the others; but the rule of the Indians was to carry
off their slain; and on this occasion, says Eager, the sur-
vivors saw the Indians after the battle engaged in this
very duty.   On the 22d of July, 1822, the bones were
buried in Goshen—Col. Hathorn, then eighty years of
age, laying the corner-stone of the monument.   Dr. Jas.
R. Wilson delivered the address, and it was estimated
that at least 15,000 people witnessed the ceremonies.
The monument bore the names of forty-four of the killed,
and the date and purposes of its erection.   In 1861 the
old monument having become much defaced, Dr. Merit
H. Cash, of Wawayanda, bequeathed four thousand dollars to the county for the purpose of procuring a new
one.   His views were carried out, and on the 22d of
July, 1862, the eighty-third anniversary of the battle,
the new monument was dedicated amid imposing ceremonies, and in presence of full as large an assemblage as

had attended that of the former. John C. Dimmick, Esq., delivered the address on the occasion.

The monument stands in the yard of the Presbyterian church at Goshen. It is of marble, each corner bearing the figure of an eagle with distended wings. On the east side is inscribed the name of the donor and date of its erection; on the north a representation of the battle scene; and on the west the names of forty-four of the killed. The whole is surmounted by a marble column bearing on the top a figure of Hope pointing upward, an appropriate memorial of the disastrous battle that cost the lives of so many of the staunch citizens of old Orange.

CHAPTER X.

In 1788, after the close of the Revolutionary war, the Legislature of the State of New York began to study more closely the wants of the people than they had done when war alone usurped their attention. A general organization act was passed, dividing the State into fourteen counties, which were subdivided into townships. Orange county was one of those formed by the general provisions of this act, but its boundaries remained the same as they had been since its first organization in 1683. It included the present county of Rockland, and extended from the Jersey line along the west side of the Hudson river to Murderer's creek, and from the mouth of Murderer's creek west along the line of Ulster county to the Delaware river.

By the provisions of this act the county was divided into the following towns, which may be said to date their first regular establishment with this year:

Cornwall,   Goshen,
Montgomery,   Newburgh,
New Windsor,   Wallkill,
Minisink,   Warwick.

Minisink, Montgomery, Newburgh and Wallkill originally included portions of the county of Ulster.

Minisink was then of considerable extent, comprising

the area now covered by the towns of Wawayanda,
Greenville, Minisink, and portions of Mount Hope and
Deerpark. In 1790 it had a population of 2,215. It
now covers less than one-third the area, yet in 1865 had
a population of 1,209. It is bounded on the south by
the State of New Jersey, east by the town of Warwick
and partly by Wawayanda, north by Wawayanda, and
west by Deerpark and part of New Jersey. The Wallkill
river and Rutger's creek form a large portion of the
southern and eastern boundary line.

The principal villages are Westtown and Unionville.
Westtown in the south-eastern, and Unionville in the
southern part, near the New Jersey State line.

Unionville is said to derive its name from the dispute
between New York and New Jersey in 1740, related in
the fourth chapter of this work. The village at the
time of the settlement of the difference, consisted of two
or three houses. It stood on the disputed territory, and
when the final boundary line was run between the two
States, it was so near the line that it took the name of
Unionville, in commemoration of the uniting of the States
in renewed friendly relations. At present it contains
a hotel, two churches, and four or five stores.

Westtown is supposed to be the oldest in date of settlement, and at the time it was founded was the only
village in the western part of the town. From this circumstance it probably derived its name. It contains a
hotel, two stores, two churches, and an academy.

Rutger's creek is the most considerable stream in the
town. It flows through it in a north-easterly direction,
furnishing the water power for a grist mill, &c., at the
village of Waterloo Mills, in the north-western corner of
the town. About three miles north of Westtown it
unites with the outlet of Binnewater pond, where it

becomes a boundary line between Wawayanda and Minisink. Its course is then south-east till it empties into the Wallkill a little below the village of Gardnersville, where it furnishes water power for a grist mill. Its name is a corruption of the word Rutky, supposed to be the name of an old Indian who formerly resided somewhere along its banks.

The first road or turnpike of any considerable magnitude in western Orange, led from the valley of the Delaware near Carpenter's Point, a short distance below Port Jervis, to Esopus, or Rondout, as it was familiarly known. It was constructed for mining purposes, and the date of its building has been lost in oblivion. It is supposed to have been built previous to the year 1664.

In 1809 a turnpike was chartered from Goshen to Carpenter's Point, where a ferry was in operation. This extends principally through the present towns of Wawayanda and Greenville, and through the villages of Denton, Brookfield, Centreville and Greenville.

In 1812 a charter was obtained for the "Goshen and Westtown Turnpike Company," passing the legislature June 1st of that year. Section first declares, "That Reuben Hopkins, Freegift Tuthill, Benjamin Strong, Stephen Jackson, James Carpenter, David M. Westcott, and all such other persons as shall associate for the purpose of making a good and sufficient turnpike road, to begin at the line that divides the States of New York and New Jersey, between the 40th and 41st mile stone, and to extend from thence to the village of Westtown, from thence to Rutger's kill near the mill of Jones and Van Cleft, from thence to the hill commonly called Pellet's Round Hill, near the edge of the Wallkill, and thence on the most eligible route to intersect the Goshen and Minisink turnpike near the village of Goshen, to be laid out by three commissioners appointed by the person administering the government of this State, shall be and hereby are erected and made a corporation and body politic, in fact and in name, by the name of the president, directors and company of the Goshen and Westtown turnpike road, and by that name shall be capable in law," to hold, purchase, or sell land, &c.; provided that the real estate owned by the company shall not exceed $2,500.

Section second appoints George D. Wickham, Stephen Jackson, Freegift Tuthill and Cotton Mathers commissioners to receive subscriptions to the stock of said company, which was to consist of seven hundred shares at $25 per share.

Section third fixes the rates of toll on said road, for every 10 miles 12½ cents for every vehicle drawn by two animals; 6 cents for every horse and rider; 12½ cents for a one-horse pleasure wagon; 25 cents for a four-wheeled carriage; and 6 cents for a sled or sleigh.

Section fourth places the quorum of directors at four; the "chord of the arch of the road" not less than twenty-four feet; and declared the act to be null and void unless the road was completed in less than four years.

In this connection I will here subjoin a law of the olden time, for the gratification of those curious in matters of ancient legislation. It was passed at an annual town meeting of the citizens of Minisink, April 1, 1790:

" WHEREAS, the raising of sheep is of great advantage to individuals and of public utility, and for the greater encouragement thereof,

" *Be it ordained and established*, by the freeholders and inhabitants of the town of Minisink, in annual town meeting assembled on the first day of April, 1790, and it is hereby ordered and established by the authority of the same, that between the twentieth day of August and the first day of November in each year thereafter, no ram or rams shall run at large in the public highways or commons in the town of Minisink, under the penalties hereafter mentioned. (Then follow the penalties, which were a forfeiture of the animal, to be sold at vendue, &c.)

"Section 2. And be it ordained and established by the authority aforesaid, that all fences in the town of Minisink in order to be lawful, shall be four feet two inches high, against all creatures belonging to persons who live in said town. (As this law has not been repealed it is presumed to be of full virtue at the present day.)

"Section 5. And be it ordered by the authority aforesaid, that a premium or reward of £3 (about $14½) shall be given to every person who shall kill a full grown wolf in the town of Minisink, and thirty shillings (about $7½) for every lesser or young wolf that can see."

The tradition is, that in those glorious old times it was the custom to intrust the votes given at town meetings to the Town Clerk, whose duty it was to count them the following day. "This," adds our informant, "often led to difficulty; for during the jollification given by the supposed successful candidates, that functionary frequently became somewhat elevated and lost the precious tickets." This however may be regarded as a "willful misrepresentation of the fact," as Irving says.

OLD FAMILIES OF MINISINK.

SAYRE.—It is not known to us what date the first resident of this name came to the town. Joshua Sayre, doubtless one of the original settlers, was elected Supervisor of the town in 1820, and was a member of the New York legislature (assembly) in 1814.

DUNNING.—The ancestor of this family was Michael Dunning, who for some time resided in Goshen. His grandson, Daniel Dunning, removed with his step-father to this town shortly after the Revolution. His uncle, Benjamin Dunning, was killed at the battle of Minisink in 1779. Benjamin Dunning, probably a descendant of the family, was elected Supervisor of the town for six consecutive years, commencing in 1814. He was also chosen a member of the New York legislature (assembly) in 1824.

BRADNER.—It is believed that at present not many descendants of the original family of this name reside in the present limits of the town. John Bradner, the first citizen of whom we find mention made, was the first Supervisor of the town after its organization in 1788. He was elected four consecutive years, commencing with 1789.

COOLEY.—The descendants of this old family, we believe, are now almost all included in the population of adjoining towns. Jonathan Cooley was first Town Clerk of the town in 1789, cotemporary with John Bradner. He held the office two years, and was elected Supervisor in 1793, which office he held four consecutive years. A descendant of his, Freegift Cooley, formerly owned the farm now owned by Mr. William H. Carpenter in Wawayanda. He is said to have been a very eccentric man, as the following incident shows: In those times, which was before the invention of stoves, it was the custom to use fire-places in which cord-wood could be used as it was first cut in the woods. One cold morning in winter, when the snow was very deep, Mr. Cooley was early engaged in dragging indoors a prodigious back-log. It happened just then that a neighboring tailor was passing by, it being a tailor's duty in those days to go from house to house and do odd jobs of mending and making apparel. Seeing Mr. Cooley struggling with the log, he concluded to assist him, and accordingly stuck his press-board in the snow and advanced to lend a helping hand. Without saying a word he took hold of one end of the log. Mr. Cooley at the same instant let go his hold, and quietly stepping behind the tailor, gave him a tremendous kick accompanied with the quaint advice, "Help when you are asked to, after this." The tailor's action in the matter is not known, but it is presumed he again took his onward way, both a sadder and wiser man.

TUTHILL.—The date of this family's emigration to this town is not known. The first citizen of the name we find mentioned in the old annals, is Freegift Tuthill, who was a member of the Goshen and Westtown Turnpike Company in 1812. Richard M. Tuthill, Jr., was elected a member of the New York Legislature (Assembly) in 1845. He was also Town Clerk in 1837, and again in 1838. He was much respected and was a very able and worthy man. His son, Mr. Charles H. Tuthill, served as Town Clerk in 1862 and in 1863. Robert C. Tuthill was also Town Clerk in 1856 and 1857. Whether all of the name are descendants of one family or not we are unable to say.

CLARK.—This family is ancient, and its descendants numerous in the towns of Wawayanda, Greenville and Minisink. The first mentioned in old records is Hulet Clark, who was first elected Town Clerk in 1819 and served two years. He was also Supervisor in 1851, 1852 and 1853. This family was the especial victims of the dysentery in the year 1825. The following members of his family died in sixteen days: (Eager's History, p. 410.)

6

Samuel J. Clark, aged 7 years, died August 17, 1825.

James M. Clark,	"	3	"	"	"	18,	"
Bertha Clark,	"	9	"	"	"	20,	"
Alfred Clark,	"	10	"	"		22,	"
Henry Clark,	"	5	"	"	"	24,	"
Mary Clark,	"	33	"	"	Sept.	2,	"

Harvey H. Clark, of Greenville, was elected Town Clerk of that town in 1855, 1859 and 1860; also, Supervisor of that town in 1865 and 1866. W. L. Clark was Town Clerk of the same town in 1856, and Alfred L. Clark in 1857. Whether originally of one common ancestry or not, we do not know.

DECKER.—This family has also representatives in Greenville and Wawayanda. The different branches are probably directly or remotely connected with Isaac Decker, who settled near Ridgebury in the year 1800.

Dewitt Decker, Esq., (of another family) was elected Supervisor of Minisink in 1860 and again in 1861. His son, Mr. Henry D. Decker, was elected Town Clerk in 1864, 1865 and 1866.

MEMBER OF PROVINCIAL CONGRESS FROM MINISINK.

| 1775 | . | . | . | John D. Coe. |

SENATORS FROM MINISINK.

| 1795 | . | . | . | John D. Coe. |

ASSEMBLYMEN FROM MINISINK.

1779–80	.	.	.	John D. Coe.
1789–90	.	.	.	John D. Coe.
1791	.	.	.	John D. Coe.
1792	.	.	.	John D. Coe.
1794	.	.	.	John D. Coe.
1812	.	.	.	Peter Holbert.
1814	.	.	.	Joshua Sayre.
1816	.	.	.	John Hallock, Jr.
1820	.	.	.	John Hallock, Jr.

1824	.	.	.	Benjamin Dunning.
1834	.	.	.	Merit H. Cash.
1835	.	.	.	Merit H. Cash.
1837	.	.	.	Merit H. Cash.
1841	.	.	.	Gideon W. Cock, Sr.
1842	.	.		Roswell Mead.
1845	.	.	.	Richard M. Tuthill, Jr.
1847	.	.	.	Joseph Davis.
1850	.	.	.	Daniel Durland.

REPRESENTATIVES IN CONGRESS OF U. S. FROM MINISINK.

1825–27—(19th Congress) John Hallock, Jr.

1827–29—(20th Congress) John Hallock, Jr.

SUPERVISORS AND TOWN CLERKS OF MINISINK FROM ITS ORGANIZATION IN 1788 TO 1866.

The first Town Meeting was held at the house of John Van Tyle, April, 1789.

SUPERVISORS.	TOWN CLERKS.
1789—John Bradner.	Jonathan Cooley.
1790—John Bradner.	Jonathan Cooley.
1791—John Bradner.	Henry Tucker.
1792—John Bradner.	Henry Tucker.
1793—Jonathan Cooley.	James Steward.
1794—Jonathan Cooley.	James Steward.
1795—Jonathan Cooley.	James Steward.
1796—Jonathan Cooley.	James Steward.
1797—Levi Van Etten.	Martiness Cuykendall.
1798—Nathan Arnout.	James Steward.
1799—Henry Tucker.	James Steward.
1800—Henry Tucker.	James Steward.
1801—Henry Tucker.	James Steward, Jr.
1802—Henry Tucker.	James Steward, Jr.
1803—Henry Tucker.	James Steward, Jr.
1804—Henry Tucker.	James Steward, Jr.
1805—Henry Tucker.	James Steward, Jr.

1806—Henry Tucker.	James Steward, Jr.
1807—Henry Tucker.	James Steward, Jr.
1808—David Christie.	James Steward, Jr.
1809—David Christie.	Increase B. Stoddard.
1810—David Christie.	Peter Holbert.
1811—Joseph Smith.	Hezekiah Taylor.
1812—Joseph Smith.	Hezekiah Taylor.
1813—Peter Holbert.	John Hallock, Jr.
1814—Benjamin Dunning.	John Hallock, Jr.
1815—Benjamin Dunning.	John Hallock, Jr.
1816—Benjamin Dunning.	John Hallock, Jr.
1817—Benjamin Dunning.	Jonathan Carpenter.
1818—Benjamin Dunning.	Jonathan Carpenter.
1819—Benjamin Dunning.	Hulet Clark.
1820—Joshua Sayre.	Hulet Clark.
1821—David Christie.	James Hulse.
1822—Benjamin Dunning.	William Evans.
1823—Benjamin Dunning.	Martin L. Mapes.
1824—Increase B. Stoddard.	Jonathan Bailey.
1825—David Christie.	Peter Holbert.
1826—David Christie.	Peter Holbert.
1827—David Christie.	James Hulse.
1828—David Christie.	James Hulse.
1829—James Hulse.	Joseph Davis.
1830—James Hulse.	Merit H. Cash.
1831—Hulet Clark.	Merit H. Cash.
1832—Merit H. Cash.	David H. Slawson.
1833—Merit H. Cash.	David H. Slawson.
1834—Joseph Davis.	John C. Owen.
1835—Isaac Cook.	Roswell Mead.
1836—Isaac Cook.	Roswell Mead.
1837—Isaac Cook.	Richard M. Tuthill.
1838—Gideon W. Cock, Sr.	Richard M. Tuthill, Jr.
1839—Gideon W. Cock, Sr.	Dewitt C. Hallock.

1840—Roswell Mead.	Erastus Stickney.
1841—Roswell Mead.	Erastus Stickney.
1842—John C. Wisner.	Henry H. Stewart.
1843—John C. Wisner.	Henry H. Stewart.
1844—Joseph Davis.	David Clark.
1845—Gabriel Horton.	Joseph M. Case.
1846—Gabriel Horton.	Stewart T. Durland.
1847—Stewart T. Durland.	Stephen Harding.
1848—Stewart T. Durland.	Lewis Armstrong.
1849—Daniel Fullerton.	William Hatch, Jr.
1850—Timothy Wood.	William Hatch, Jr.
1851—Hulet Clark.	Henry C. Halsey.
1852—Hulet Clark.	Samuel B. Elston.
1853—Hulet Clark.	Isaac Winters.
1854—Albert A. Seymour.	Simeon M. Coykendall.
1855—Albert A. Seymour.	Simeon M. Coykendall.
1856—Joseph M. Case.	Robert C. Tuthill.
1857—Joseph M. Case.	Robert C. Tuthill.
1858—John C. Wisner.	Jacob P. Snook.
1859—John C. Wisner.	Jacob P. Snook.
1860—Dewitt Decker.	John R. Halstead.
1861—Dewitt Decker.	John R. Halstead.
1862—Joseph M. Case.	Charles H Tuthill.
1863—Joseph M. Case.	Charles H. Tuthill.
1864—Joseph M. Case.	Henry D. Decker.
1865—Joseph M. Case.	Henry D. Decker.
1866—Joseph M. Case.	Henry D. Decker.

The number of acres of land assessed in the town in 1865, was 14,045 ; assessed value thereof, $512,209, or about $36 47 per acre ; personal property, $140,989.

CHAPTER XI.

In 1798 the county of Rockland was set off from Orange by act of the legislature ; and in order to maintain the size of Orange county, five towns from Ulster were incorporated into its limits, making it of its present dimensions. The present town of Deerpark was thus formed principally from the town of Mamakating, in Ulster county. Eager says the name arose from the following circumstance : A man by the name of McDaniel, one of the early settlers, owned a small tract of land somewhere within its limits, which he enclosed with a fence made of brush and small trees lopped together. Some of his neighbors to ridicule it called it McDaniel's "deer-park;" and the name became so familiar that the whole vicinity soon went by the same cognomen by which the town is now known. The most of the town is included in the limits of the old Minisink patent, which also covers a large portion of the town of Minisink, in conjunction with the Wawayanda patent. As has been made known in the previous chapters of this work, this portion of Orange was one of the earliest settled ; the fertile valleys of the Delaware and Neversink attracting attention from the very first visitors of that region. In 1800, two years after the formation of the town of Deerpark, it had a population of 955. In 1855 it had increased to 5,504, and in 1865 to 7,417. It is bounded on the north by Sullivan county, west by Pennsylvania, south by Pennsylvania and New Jersey, and east by Greenville and Mount Hope. Mongaup river or creek forms the boundary line on the north-west, the Delaware river on the south and south-west, and the Shawangunk mountain on the east.

The principal streams are, the Neversink, flowing through the town in a southerly direction ; the Bashus' kill, also flowing south ; and Ouwe (Old) Dam kill, Sparrowbush creek, Grassy Swamp brook, Fall brook and other streams. The Neversink is supposed to be an old Indian name, though the true appellation, according to the Indian tongue, was Mahackemeck. The former name is doubtless an allusion to the character of the stream, which has a current of such rapidity that, unless of very heavy bulk, articles thrown upon its surface will float some distance before sinking : hence are said to "never sink." Bashus' kill is named after an old squaw by the name of Bashee, who is said to have resided for a long time on its banks near the present village of Westbrookville, and was very friendly to the white people of that region. These streams furnish abundant water power, and as a consequence saw mills, grist mills, &c., are conveniently interspersed throughout the town. Eager says, (p. 370) that the first attempt to grind grain was made by an old settler named Jacob Cuddeback, (or Codebeck,) who built a small mill on a spring brook near his house ; one of the original millstones of which is still to be seen in the cellar of Peter E. Gumaer. Two mills were early erected on Ouwe Dam kill, (Old Dam brook,) also one on the Neversink river, near Cuddebackville, in the year 1770, by Jacob R. De Witt, according to the same authority. Several others were located near where Port Jervis now stands.

The principal villages of the town are Port Jervis and Cuddebackville. Westbrookville, Huguenot, Bolton and Gumaer's, are thriving places.

Port Jervis may be said to have been founded in the year 1826, the date of the construction of the Delaware and Hudson canal through the town, to which event this thriving village may be said to be indebted for its origin. It is named after the superintendent who attended the building of the canal, one Mr. Jervis, who made it his place of business for some time. The first merchants in the village were Gilbert F. Mondon, Stephen St. John and Benjamin Dodge. The two last named were in partnership at first. These men, with Dr. Conklin, are said to have been the first to abandon the sale of spirituous liquors when the agitation of the temperance question commenced. In 1859 the village contained thirteen stores, nine hotels, two tobacco manufactories, grist mills, and numerous representatives of the different professional pursuits, besides the extensive machine shops of the Erie Railway company, which are well worthy of a visit from those curious in matters of machinery, or who like to view the giant iron horse at rest by the dozen in this vast stable—the engine house.

The village being the western end of the eastern division of the Erie Railway, which was built through the town a few years after the Delaware and Hudson canal, has no doubt greatly enhanced its prosperity. The small village of Germantown, or as it was formerly called, Honesdale, a short distance north-west on the canal, may now properly be styled a part of Port Jervis, since the whole line of the canal in that vicinity is a continuous village.

Cuddebackville is in the north-eastern part of the town on the line of the canal. It is named in honor of an old settler, Jacob Cuddeback, one of the original owners of a patent given in the year 1697, for the land in what was called the Peenpack valley. One of his descendants, Col. William Cuddeback, owned the site of the village at the date of the building of the canal, which was the origin of the village. It now has two or three stores, two churches and a hotel.

Westbrookville is a small village, north-east from Cuddebackville, also on the canal, which gave rise to it. A store and hotel comprise its business portion, and it is named after John Westbrook, who kept a sort of store or tavern at this same place before the Revolution, and whose descendants for a long time resided near it.

Huguenot is a small village between Port Jervis and Gumaer's, on the canal. It is chiefly noted for the mineral springs lately discovered near it, and the splendid hotel erected there. It is named after the Protestant refugees from France, many of whom settled in the valley, and were called Huguenots. It has a grist mill, stores, &c.

Gumaer's is a small collection of houses on the canal, north of Huguenot, has a store and hotel, and is the residence of Gumaer Brothers, descendants of one of the original patentees of Peenpack, in 1697.

Bolton is a small place in the south-western part of the town, on the canal, and is named after John Bolton, an original member of the canal company.

Deerpark boasts of two suspension bridges, which are in truth beautiful evidences of the triumph of science, and perfect imitations of their great prototype, the

6*

Niagara suspension bridge. One is located between Gumaer's and Cuddebackville, across the Neversink river, and the other between Gumaer's and the mines, across the same stream. The latter was built by Gumaer Brothers at their own expense.

The wooden bridge across the Delaware, just above Port Jervis, is also worthy of notice as a very good one of its class.

OLD FAMILIES OF DEERPARK.

GUMAER.—Previous to emigration from France this name is said to have been spelled *Guymard*, and in the adoption of a name for the new post office at " the mines," thus came in use. For some time after the emigration it was spelled *Germar*, and this has since been modernized to the present mode of pronunciation, *Gumaer*. Peter Gumaer, the ancestor of the family, came to the town in the year 1690. He belonged to the branch of Protestants known as Huguenots, some 50,-000 of whom were driven into exile by the revoking of the famous Edict of Nantes. He is supposed to have left France, his native land, about 1685 or 1686, starting with the intention of going to England. He however changed his mind in regard to the latter determination, and came to America. In 1697, (October 14th,) together with six others, he purchased a patent of twelve hun- dred acres in what was called by the Indians " Peen- pack "—tradition says at a cost of from two to four shil- lings per acre. This patent soon after came into pos- session of the patentees, viz.: Peter Gumaer, Jacob Cuddeback, one of the Swartouts, and a settler named Harmanus Van Inwegen. It has mostly remained in possession of their descendants to the present time. Mr. Gumaer was a very active participant in the events

of those early times, one of the principal forts for defense against the Indians being located at his house.
He brought the first fanning mill to Minisink ever seen
in this section, about 1750 or 1760. He married a Miss
Swartout, and had seven children—six daughters and
one son. This son, Peter, was born November 15, 1708.
He married Charity DeWitt, daughter of Jacob DeWitt,
of Rochester, Ulster county. They had four sons and
two daughters—Peter, born February 19, 1732; Jacob,
born December 12, 1739; Ezekiel, born December 29,
1742; Elias, born January 22, 1748; Esther, born Jan.
2, 1730; Margaret, born May 12, 1736; Mary, born July
16, 1745; and Elizabeth, born Dec 5, 1750, but who died
at the age of two years. Of these, Ezekiel married
Naomi Low, daughter of Abraham Low, of Rochester,
Ulster county, in the year 1770. They had but two
children, both sons: Abraham, born October 3, 1783,
who died at the age of twelve years, and Peter E., born
May 28, 1771, now living. Peter E. Gumaer, Esq.,
married Esther Cuddeback, October 10, 1813, and has
had seven children: Morgan, born January 27, 1815;
Ezekiel, born May 10, 1817; Jacob C. E., born October
18, 1820; Peter L., born January 29, 1827; Naomi, born
January 29, 1830; Andrew J., born November 4, 1833,
and Esther H., born August 30, 1835. This venerable
gentleman gave us these particulars personally a short
time since. As will be seen by the date of his birth, he
is verging on toward a longevity of life seldom equaled,
almost a century of years having passed over his head.
His eye is still bright and his voice clear and strong.
He remembers the Indians that frequented the valley
before the Revolutionary war; one in particular, named
Scott, who made him a bow and arrows at the fort at
his father's, when he was a little boy. He saw the peo-

ple going to the battle of Minisink, and recollects one
John Waller, about whom great uneasiness was felt by
his friends, he being absent some two or three days after
the battle; but who finally returned safe and sound,
with several deerskins on his back, he having been
hunting on his way home. The same individual stood
close by Capt. Cuddeback in the battle. A bullet came
whistling through his coat, at which the Captain remarked, "John, hadn't you better stand a little back?
They shoot d—d good." "No," he replied, "I want to
get a chance at them." Captain Cuddeback's advice to
the settlers on pursuing the Indians, was to attack them
secretly in the night, but not being used to that mode
of warfare they were afraid of shooting each other in
the dark. They finally determined to attack them while
crossing the river. This plan might have succeeded
had not Captain Tyler's gun accidentally went off, thus
apprising the Indians of their being pursued. Mr.
Gumaer recollects Captain Cuddeback's narration of his
escape after the battle. He says Cuddeback was a
powerful man physically, one of his feats of strength
being the raising of a fifty-six pound weight attached to
each finger and thumb of his right hand, making in all
two hundred and eighty pounds, at arm's length. He
was Captain of the fort located at his father's for some
time.

Mrs. Gumaer, also living, has been her husband's companion in the bonds of conjugal felicity fifty-three years,
and like him, remembers back to a time when the principal
implements used in agricultural operations were rudely
fashioned and mostly of wood; when the clothes were
altogether of home manufacture; when the men wore
their hair long, and had it powdered and tied up in
queues like the Chinese: and when the grain intended

for bread had to be pounded in a stone mortar with a round stone about eighteen inches in length and three or four in diameter, by hand—a work mostly performed by the women; having, as she said, " many a time pounded corn till her hands were blistered." Her memory is full of old-time incidents, one of which, relating to the naming of Bashus' kill, is as follows: An old squaw by the name of Bashee, and her husband, lived for many years by this stream. They were very friendly to the whites and lived in content long after their tribe had gone west. The old chief was a good hunter, and was frequently accompanied by his wife, who carried the game on such occasions. During one of these excursions he shot a large deer, and tying the two legs fast to a stick, old Bashee took it on her shoulder and started homeward, he following slowly along the path. Her way was over the stream, which was crossed by a log reaching from bank to bank. In crossing, she slipped from the log, and the stick caught her fast by the neck so that it was impossible to free herself. Her husband shortly found her dead, with the deer hanging across the log—and that is the way it came to be called Bashus' kill, or more properly Bashee's kill.

CUDDEBACK.—This name was at first spelled Codeback, but English usage soon changed it to Cuddeback. Jacob Cuddeback, the ancestor of the family, was a countryman of Gumaer's, and came with him to America. They first landed in Maryland, and being short of funds, labored for a time till they procured the wherewithal to enable them to emigrate to Minisink. They were partners in almost all transactions; and either in the city, or in one of the counties on the east side of the Hudson, (says Eager,) both entered into the interesting state of matrimony with the daughters of a Dutch family named Swartout. Three members of the Swartout family accompanied their newly-made relatives to the Minisink Region. These were Thomas Swartout, Bernardus Swartout and Anthony Swartout, all of whom were concerned in the purchase of the Peenpack Patent. Cuddeback built the first grist mill erected in the present limits of the town. He was much noted for the part taken in the New Jersey boundary dispute. He is said to have been well educated, of extensive historical knowledge, and so well versed in the Scriptures that theological questions were always left to his decision. He was the one selected to go to the Governor to procure the patent on behalf of the purchasers in 1697, which mission he successfully accomplished. He lived to be about one hundred years old, and his faculties were good to the day of his death. His descendants are quite numerous, and have always occupied conspicuous places in the history of the Minisink Region, the scene of their daring ventures, hair-breath escapes, and perils untold of the Indian wars and Revolutionary struggle, and of their prosperity in the better times since then.

SWARTOUT.—The ancestors of this family were of Dutch origin, and came to this town with Gumaer and Cuddeback in 1690. They were all three interested in the Peenpack Patent, but Eager says that but one of them kept his share. Whether it was Thomas, Anthony, or Bernardus, that refused to sell, we are not informed. They were said to be all large, powerful men, and well fitted for the hardships of a pioneer's life in the wilderness. One of them in 1730 was major of the militia of Orange county. He resided on the disputed territory between New York and New Jersey, and was once dispossessed by the Jersey claimants; an affair that called out all his neighbors in order to reinstate him, as related in a previous chapter. Cornelius Swartout and Gerardus Swartout, a son of the Major, were at the capture of Fort Montgomery by the British, but escaped. This family bore an important part in all the struggles and hardships of those troublous times, and their descendants may well point proudly to the record. This family, nearly all, we believe, now spell their name Swartwout.

VAN INWEGEN.—Nothing of the nationality of this ancient family is known, but as most of the early settlers in the Minisink Region were German, and the name sounds like those of that derivation, we may safely set it down as coming from that nation. Harmanus Van Inwegen we first find mentioned as becoming part owner of the twelve hundred acre patent, doubtless the buyer of the shares sold by the Swartouts. Eager says he married a daughter of one of the Swartouts. He is represented as being a powerful man, so much so that the strongest Indians were unable to cope with him. He took a very prominent part in the border war with New Jersey, and became a member of the committee of safety organized in the Minisink Region in 1777. A young man named Gerardus Van Inwegen was killed at the capture of Fort Montgomery, but whether he was a son of Harmanus or not we do not know. The citizens of Deerpark by that name, are doubtless mostly descendants of his.

WESTBROOK.—We know but little of the origin of this family. The original ancestor of the family in this town was John Westbrook, whom we first find mentioned in the old annals as keeping a store where Westbrookville now stands, which was a celebrated resort for the Indian trade previous to and during the old French war of 1755. Major and Johannes Westbrook, relatives

of his, are said by Eager to have been captured by the
Jerseymen, at the old Mahackemeck church, during the
border troubles, about 1764 or 1767, and confined for
some time in the old Jersey Colony prison, but was
soon released. They appear to have been men of some
importance in those times.

DECKER.—The progenitor of this family settled in
what was known as the "lower neighborhood," about
the same time, or shortly after the settlement of the
Peenpack Patent by Gumaer and Cuddeback. His name
was John Decker, and he kept a store or tavern for some
years before and after the French and Indian war. It
was near his house that Tom Quick is said to have
killed Mushwink, the Indian. This was after the close
of the war. Mushwink was among the Indians who
returned to the settlement, (Quinlan's Life of Tom
Quick, p. 46), and one day happened to be at Decker's
tavern pretty drunk, and boasting of his exploits.
Quick was present, and in order to irritate him the
savage gave an account of his helping to kill Thomas
Quick, Sr., and exhibited the silver sleeve buttons worn
by the victim when killed. This aroused Quick's feelings, and catching a loaded musket from its place over
the mantle, he ordered the Indian to leave the room.
The Indian saw he was in earnest, and obeyed with a
crestfallen air. Quick followed him toward Carpenter's
Point about a mile, when he exclaimed, "Indian dog,
you'll kill no more white men," and instantly shot him
in the back between the shoulders. The savage leaped
two or three feet in the air and fell dead. A fort was
located at Decker's by the committee of safety in 1778.
It was captured by the Indians under Brandt in 1779.
Major John Decker, according to Eager, had a narrow
escape from the same body of Indians; and his wife and

children fled to Mr. James Finch's, east of the Shawan-gunk, for safety.

DEWITT.—There were four brothers of the name, who first emigrated from Holland. (Eager, p. 396.) One settled in the town of Hurley, one in Rochester, and one in Napanoch, Ulster county; the fourth is supposed to have settled in Duchess county. Jacob R. DeWitt, who settled in this town, was a son of the one who settled at Napanoch. Miss Mary DeWitt, sister of Jacob R., married Gen. James Clinton, of New Windsor. They had four children. DeWitt Clinton, the illustrious states-man, was one of them; and Eager says Deerpark is enti-tled to the honor of giving him a birthplace, owing to the following incident:

"In February, 1769, James Clinton, with his lady, came to the fort at DeWitt's, on a visit to see her brother, Capt. Jacob Rutson DeWitt. A violent snow storm came on which lasted some days, and when it abated Mrs. Clinton was found to be in such an inter-esting situation as to make it imprudent to return home. They remained at the fort six weeks, and during the interval DeWitt Clinton was born."

Moses DeWitt, Jacob R. DeWitt's eldest son, was a person of very agreeable manners, and well liked by the Indians, who deeply lamented his death. He surveyed the boundary line between New York and New Jersey in 1787.

VAN AUKEN.—The first resident of this town by the name, is believed to have been Abraham Van Auken, but from whence he came and the date of settlement is unknown. A fort was erected at the house of Daniel Van Auken, one of his descendants, in the "lower neighborhood," by order of the committee of safety in 1778. Jeremiah Van Auken, doubtless a member of the

same family, was killed during Brandt's invasion of Minisink in 1779.

MILLS.—This family is very ancient, and it is proba-
ble that the persons of that name throughout Mount
Hope, Wawayanda, Deerpark and other towns, are
branches of the same family, though in many cases the
connection has been lost. In an old copy of *The Gazette*
(if we mistake not) mention is made of the death of a
citizen named Mills, in Connecticut, in the year 1726,
aged ninety-five years, and " who was born in America."
This would place the date of his birth at 1631, just
eleven years after the landing of the pilgrims at Ply-
mouth; so we may conclude his parents to have come
over in the Mayflower. In 1656, "Thompson's History
of Long Island " mentions the names of a number of
persons from Milford, (Connecticut, we presume,) who
signed a petition to Governor Stuyvesant asking leave to
settle at a place called Jamaica, L. I. This was granted
and the settlement commenced. One of the petitioners
was named George Mills. Timothy Mills, a few years
afteward removed from Jamaica, and settled at a place
called Mills' Pond, Suffolk county, L. I. By his first wife
he had two children, and by his second, eleven children.
Of these Jonathan was born October 23, 1710. He married Ruth Rutgard, by whom he had six children. Of
these Jacob was born December 23, 1746. He married
Catherine Denton, daughter of Samuel Denton, of Long
Island, by whom he had twelve children. He came
from Mills' Pond to Little Britain in Orange county,
where he followed the business of a tanner for some
time, and from where he removed to the town of Wallkill, near Scotchtown, at a very early date. One of his
children, William Wickham Mills, afterward married the
only daughter of Wickham Denton, Esq., of L. I.

Another, Samuel Mills, married Miss Elizabeth Stitt, by whom he had fourteen children. Of these, Rev. Samuel W. Mills, of Port Jervis, is the ninth. One of the daughters (lately deceased) married Theodore J. Denton, Esq., of Wawayanda.

CLAUSON.—This family originally settled at an early date in the town of Minisink; but has become so scattered that we believe it has few if any of the name at present in the town. Aaron Clauson, grandfather of George Clauson, Esq., of Port Jervis, came from Newark, N. J., and settled near Unionville in 1793–4. In 1797 he purchased a farm of Daniel Myers at that place. On this farm his son, Elias Clauson, lived for seventy years, or until his death, which occurred a few years ago. This gentleman was possessed of numerous incidents concerning Daniel Myers; who, it will be recollected, was a great hunter and Indian slayer. On one occasion he was at the house of Mr. Myers, who was then an old man, but still an unerring marksman with the rifle. A bird of curious shape was seen flying through the air overhead, and old Mr. Myers brought out his rifle, remarking that he would find out what it was. It was so high as to look about the size of a man's hat, but, so true was the old man's aim, that the crack of his rifle brought it whirling to the ground, when it was found to be an eagle of the largest size. The Indians on another occasion surprised the old man while splitting rails. He acknowledged himself a prisoner, but requested them to help open a log before taking him off. This they agreed to, knowing he could not get away. So they ranged themselves on both sides of the log and took hold to pull it apart while he drove the wedges. No sooner had they signified their readiness, than a well directed blow knocked out the wedge and the log closed together, catching every one by their fingers. He then leisurely knocked them in the head with the axe one by one. (Some say this was Tom Quick, but we believe Daniel Myers to be the man.)

VAN ETTEN.—Anthony Van Etten is the first resident of the town of whom we have any account. He resided in the "lower neighborhood," near Decker's, in 1779. He was a man of much note among the early settlers. Thomas Van Etten, Jr., represented western Orange in the legislature with ability, some years since.

VAN VLIET (or VAN FLEET.)—James Van Vliet is the first resident of the town, of the name, and narrowly escaped from the Indians with his family during Brandt's invasion, 1779. John Van Vliet for a long time owned the land afterward owned by Michael Van Vliet and Solomon Van Vliet.

WESTFALL.—The first record of this family shows it to have been located in the "lower neighborhood" in 1755, when a fort was erected at their residence to protect the settlers from the Indians. It was an important position, and the Indians tried many times to surprise the place. This family was the first attacked by Brandt in 1779, where one man was killed. (Eager, p. 386.)

Henry Cortright, Solomon Davis, Benjamin DuPuy, Solomon Cole, William Cole, Peter Cuykendall, Abraham Low and Evert Hornbeck were old settlers, many of whose descendants are still comprised in the enterprising population of the town. The citizens of Port Jervis may well remember with gratitude the liberality of Col. Samuel Fowler, of later days, who may well be considered a patron of the place and a great promoter of its prosperity. Some of the finest buildings in the village were built by him.

I will notice here, as it may not be out of place to

record the notice of a personage so well known to the early inhabitants of this section, Ben Shanks, a native Indian chief; in person tall, slender and athletic, in fact said to be the tallest Indian ever seen on the Delaware; from which circumstance he probably derived his English name, his true name being Huycon. His hair was jet black and clubbed behind, his forehead high and wrinkled, his eyes of a fiery brown color, and sunk deep in their sockets, his nose pointed and aquiline, his front teeth remarkably broad, prominent and white, his cheeks hollow and furrowed; in a word, Ben Shanks, when arrayed in all the warlike habiliments of his tribe, presented one of the most frightful specimens of human nature that the eye could rest upon. (Quinlan's Life of Tom Quick.) He was well known throughout Orange and Ulster, and dreaded for his cruel and bloodthirsty disposition in time of war. The most cruel murder he was concerned in, was perpetrated near the close of the Revolutionary war. Colonel Johannis Jansen, a noted patriot, whom Shanks had often worked for when a boy, lived in the north-eastern part of the town of Shawangunk, Ulster county. Christopher Mentze, his nearest neighbor, was a German inhabiting a comfortable log house three-quarters of a mile distant in a westerly direction. His son, John Mentze, had married a daughter of John George Mack, who lived on the other side of the mountain. A few months before the tragedy, a young lady named Hannah had come from New York and was visiting at Mr. Mentze's, who was her uncle. She is described as being about eighteen years of age, and a most decidedly lovely and interesting young lady. Being of an industrious disposition, she had been hired to spin for Col. Jansen's family, spending her Sabbaths at her uncle's.

One Monday morning in September, Colonel Jansen, while going to a barrack near his barn, was surprised by two Indians who attempted to take him prisoner. He managed to escape from them, and ran for the house shouting murder, pursued by one Indian who got so near him that he tried to catch hold of him. The Colonel got inside the door first and shut it, but did not have time to bolt it. The Indian endeavored to push the door open, but in the struggle the Colonel proved the stronger, and the attempt failed. The savage then attempted to break open the door with a broad-axe which was lying on the porch. The Colonel frightened him away by calling loudly for his musket and pistols. These his wife brought, and the Colonel determined to defend the house at all hazards. His wife raised a window sash for the purpose of closing the blinds so as to darken the room, but was frightened away by a man disguised as an Indian, but whose blue eyes at once revealed the Tory. The Colonel then retired to the upper part of the house with his family, and the assailants soon broke into the lower rooms. The Colonel's three female slaves were captured and placed near the door under charge of Ben Shanks, while the Tory and three other savages searched for valuables. Just at this time one of the slaves saw Hannah coming through the gateway near the barn, to resume her spinning at the Colonel's. The slave motioned to her in the most forcible manner to go back, that she was in danger and must not come to the house; but the poor girl not understanding her meaning, walked leisurely into the kitchen. When she comprehended her danger, her terror was extreme. She wrung her hands in agony, and with one of the slaves uttered the most moving entreaties for life. But the unfeeling monsters compelled her with the uplifted tomahawk to take a place with the slaves. Then gathering up the spoils, they ordered their prisoners to advance, one of them leading the way across the fields toward the mountain, and leaving Col. Jansen in possesion of his house.

While these events were taking place, Mr. Mack, with his daughter Elsie, a young lady of eighteen, had been to visit his son-in-law, John Mentze, and to take back their winter clothing which they had been in the habit of leaving at Mr. Mentze's when not needed, as Mack's dwelling was more exposed to Indian and Tory depredations. They were now on their way home across the mountain, accompanied by John Mentze, following an Indian path through the woods, the nearest habitation over the mountain being nine miles. After going about four miles they reached the foot of a precipitous ledge near the summit of the mountain, and stopped to rest, Mack remarking to his son-in-law, as he sat down to light his pipe, that he had gone far enough and might return. While they were talking, Elsie climbed to the summit of the precipice to enjoy the view, which comprised a large portion of Orange and Ulster counties. Suddenly their horses seemed frightened at something in the bushes not far from where they had been tied. They looked round for the cause, and the old man seeing them first, cried out, "They are Indians." Mentze raised on tiptoe, and looking over the laurels, replied, "No; it is a Tory with negroes." Almost as soon as he spoke however he saw the frightful visage of Shanks, with the three negroes behind him, creeping toward them under cover of the laurel bushes, while the Tory and other Indians had gained the path below them to cut off their retreat. Being unarmed, he saw there was no safety but in flight, and immediately fled toward the horses, running under the neck of one of them, and toward the bank of a brook. As he turned down the bank of the brook, he heard Elsie give a heart-rending shriek, but knew he could do nothing to aid the doomed girl, and not daring to waste his time, he leaped into the brook, a distance of some fifteen feet, in doing which he severely sprained his ankle. Unheeding the pain he threw off his now water-soaked shoes, and fled down the rocky bottom of the brook and across the fields to Mr. Thomas Jansen's, a brother of the Colonel. Seeing persons passing, he halloed loudly and was heard. A party of friends quickly volunteered, and Mentze procuring his faithful rifle, led the way regardless of his bruised and swollen ankle. On arriving at the place of the attack a bundle of clothes was found, but nothing could be seen of Mr. Mack or his daughter. Tracks were found leading in a westerly direction, toward the aforementioned brook. They were followed, and on ascending about ten paces up a gentle declivity on the other side of the brook, the objects of their search were exposed to view. At the foot of a rock oak tree, the old man lay upon his hands and knees, dead, and scalped in the most horrible manner. From his position it was evident he had struggled long in the agonies of death. His head hung down between his shoulders, and his hands were clenched and filled with leaves. About five feet further up lay his daughter, stretched at full length upon the bank, her clothing properly arranged, and her inanimate form scalped in the same terrible manner. A rude bier was constructed, and their remains tenderly and mournfully carried home for proper interment. Mentze was so overcome by the affecting scene that he had to be supported homeward by the strong arms of his sympathizing friends, He remembered that Hannah, captured at Col. Jansen's, was not with Shanks' band when he saw them, and search was instantly made for her. The next day, as they were about giving up the search, a dog belonging to the party was observed to direct his course to a lonely field near the Colonel's house, and on following him they soon came in sight of the mangled corpse of her whom they sought. Like her friend Elsie, she too had been scalped, and the bleeding skull excited feelings of horror in those who came to witness the scene. She too was transported in silence to the humble mansion of her venerable uncle, and from thence in due season to that solitary bourne from whence no traveler returns.

Shanks after this affair never ventured again in that neighborhood. He however made his appearance after the war at Cochecton, in company with Canope, an Indian of that place. They were warned by the whites not to remain long in the vicinity, but disregarding the caution, they proceeded up the Delaware to fish and hunt. Finally they got acquainted with a man named Ben Haines, who lived near Handsome Eddy, and concluded to make his house their home. Haines managed to send word to Tom Quick and Cobe Shimer (an acquaintance of the two ladies murdered on the Shawangunk,) at Minisink, and they proceeded to Haines' house secretly, for the purpose of trapping the Indians. They placed themselves in ambush near the bank of the river, and Haines, understanding their position, enticed the Indians to a favorable spot under pretense of its being better fishing. Quick and Shimer fired at them—Quick wounding Canope, while Shimer missed Shanks entirely. Haines knocked Canope in the head with a pine knot. Shanks fled, and was pursued by Quick some distance, but escaped by reason of superior speed. He passed

7

through Cochecton afterward on his way west, breathing vengeance against the white man, and was never more seen along the Delaware. (Quinlan's Life of Tom Quick.)

TOM QUICK.—The ancestors of this celebrated person were among the earliest settlers in Ulster county, having emigrated to that section some time previous to the year 1700. Tom's father, as has been previously stated, was murdered by the Indians in an extremely barbarous manner; an event that shaped the future of Tom's life. This took place near where Milford now stands, on the Pennsylvania side of the river. Tom was a boy at the time, and as affairs were then in an extremely unsettled state, it being just previous to the commencement of the old French and Indian war, he had a fine opportunity to revenge the death of his father. He took to the woods, followed hunting, fishing and trapping for a living, and grew to man's stature almost an Indian in appearance. His antipathy to that race grew with his years, and he was never known to miss an opportunity of killing an Indian, young or old. He once slew an Indian chief, squaw, and their children, in a canoe on the Neversink. When reproached with killing the children he replied, " Nits make lice." The Indians tried hard to get him in their power, and twice took him prisoner, but his good fortune enabled him to escape each time. They once stole the bell of a cow owned by his relative, where he was staying, and hid with it among the brush, knowing he was in the habit of driving up the cow at night. When he came out to look for her, they jingled the bell gently to entice him to the spot; but Tom mistrusted something, by the bell being rung so long in one place, and accordingly crept around behind them unseen, and with his trusty rifle killed one and severely wounded another. He died peacefully at an advanced age, regretting only that he had not quite killed an even hundred of the hated race.

MEMBER OF PROVINCIAL CONGRESS FROM DEERPARK.

1775 . . . David Pye.

MEMBERS OF CONVENTIONS TO FORM STATE CONSTITUTION
FROM DEERPARK.

1777 . . . David Pye.
1846 . . . Lewis Cuddeback.

MEMBERS OF COLONIAL ASSEMBLY FROM DEERPARK.

1752 . . . Moses DePue, Jr.
1759 . . . Moses DePue, Jr.

MEMBERS OF STATE SENATE FROM DEERPARK.

1791 . . . David Pye.
1792 . David Pye.
1793 . . David Pye.
1794 . . . David Pye.

MEMBERS OF COUNCIL OF APPOINTMENT FOR STATE SENATORS
FROM DEERPARK.

1784 . . Jacobus Swartout.
1786 . . . Jacobus Swartout.
1792 . . . David Pye.

MEMBERS OF ASSEMBLY FROM DEERPARK.

1795 . . . David Pye.
1796 . . David Pye.
1803 . . . James Finch, Jr.
1010 . . . James Finch, Jr.
1814 . . . James Finch, Jr.
1815 . . . James Finch, Jr.
1816 . . . James Finch.
1817 . . . James Finch.

1820	.	.	. James Finch, Jr.
1824	.	.	. James Finch, Jr.
1830	.	.	. Abraham Cuddeback.
1833	.	.	. James Finch.
1836	.	.	. Thomas Van Etten, Jr.
1841	.	.	. Lewis Cuddeback.
1852	.	.	. Abraham J. Cuddeback.
1855	.	.	. James Bennet.

The town book previous to 1854 appears to have been lost, as the writer with the assistance of Mr. W. E. Haggerty, the present Town Clerk, searched the office for it thoroughly without avail. The following list of the names of the Supervisors and Town Clerks we derived from loose papers in the office, and is imperfect; but until the lost records can be found or replaced, there will necessarily be a blank in regard to some of the early town proceedings.

The first town meeting after the organization of the town appears to have been held May 2, 1799, and the following gentlemen acted as inspectors of election, viz.: James Finch, Jr., William Deem, William Young, Joseph Smith and Elias Gumaer. In 1801 the town meeting was held at the house of Samuel Watkins.

NAMES OF THE SUPERVISORS AND TOWN CLERKS OF DEER-PARK, FROM ITS ORGANIZATION TO THE PRESENT TIME.

SUPERVISORS.	TOWN CLERKS.
1799—James Finch, Jr.	—— ——
1800—James Finch, Jr.	—— ——
1801—James Finch.	Enoch Tuthill.
1802— —— ——	—— ——
1803— —— ——	—— ——
1804— —— ——	—— ——
1805— —— ——	—— ——
1806—Peter E. Gumaer.	James Finch, Jr.

SUPERVISORS.	TOWN CLERKS.
1807—James Finch.	Peter E. Gumaer.
1808—James Finch.	Peter E. Gumaer.
1809—James Finch, Jr.	Stephen Farnum.
1810—Peter E. Gumaer.	Stephen Farnum.
1811—Peter E. Gumaer.	Stephen Farnum.
1812—Peter E. Gumaer.	Stephen Farnum.
1813—Peter E. Gumaer.	Stephen Farnum.
1814—Peter E. Gumaer.	Stephen Farnum.
1815—James Finch, Jr.	Charles Murray.
1816—James Finch, Jr.	Charles Murray.
1817—Abraham Cuddeback.	Charles Murray.
1818—James Finch, Jr.	Stephen Farnum.
1819—James Finch, Jr.	Stephen Farnum.
1820—Abraham Cuddeback.	Stephen Farnum.
1821— —— ——	—— ——
1822— —— ——	—— ——
1823— —— ——	—— ——
1824—David G. Finch.	Joseph Conklin.
1825—Peter E. Gumaer.	—— ——
1826—Peter E. Gumaer.	—— ——
1827—Philip Swartout.	Benj. Van Inwegen.
1828—Philip Swartout.	—— ——
1829—Benjamin Cuddeback.	Benj. Van Inwegen.
1830—Levi Van Inwegen.	—— ——
1831— —— ——	—— ——
1832— —— ——	—— ——
1833— —— ——	—— ——
1834— —— ——	—— ——
1835—Lewis Cuddeback.	—— ——
1836—Lewis Cuddeback.	John S. Van Inwegen.
1837—Lewis Cuddeback.	John S. Van Inwegen.
1838—George Burns.	Peter Cuddeback.
1839—Levi Van Etten.	Peter Cuddeback.

SUPERVISORS.	TOWN CLERKS.
1840—Levi Van Etten.	Peter Cuddeback.
1841— —— ——	—— ——
1842—Lewis Van Inwegen.	John S. Van Inwegen.
1843— —— ——	—— ——
1844— —— ——	—— ——
1845— —— ——	—— ——
1846— —— ——	—— ——
1847— —— ——	—— ——
1848—Peter Van Inwegen.	Peter G. Van Inwegen.
1849—David Swartout.	J. B. Crawford.
1850—James Van Fleet.	—— ——
1851—Samuel Fowler.	Peter G. Van Inwegen.
1852— —— ——	F. W. Lockwood.
1853— ——— ——	F. W. Lockwood.
1854—James Bennet.	Waltemire Westbrook.
1855—Eli Van Inwegen.	Andrew Conger.
1856—Eli Van Inwegen.	Joseph H. Knowlton.
1857—Peter Cuddeback.	Dayton T. Cox.
1858—John Van Etten.	George Brodhead.
1859—John Van Etten.	George Brodhead.
1860—Solomon Van Etten.	George Brodhead.
1861—Solomon Van Etten.	Charles W. Douglass.
1862—Orville J. Brown.	Edgar A. Wells.
1863—Franklin R. Brodhead.	Dayton T. Cox.
1864—Franklin R. Brodhead.	Francis R. Fossard.
1865—Franklin R. Brodhead.	George Clauson.
1866—Franklin R. Brodhead.	William E. Haggerty.

The number of acres of land assessed in the town in 1865, was 34,225; assessed value, $1,192,520; personal property, $241,600.

CHAPTER XII.

This town was erected by an act of the State Legislature in 1825. It was formed from parts of the towns of Minisink, Wallkill and Deerpark, and was first called Calhoun, in honor of John C. Calhoun, the celebrated statesman of South Carolina. His views, policy, and patriotic course as Secretary of War during the contest with Great Britain in 1812, had rendered him a very popular man at the time, and thus the town came to be named after him. It went by this name till 1831 or 1832, when the inhabitants suddenly discovered his principles of public government to disagree with theirs. No time was lost in endeavoring to obliterate his memory from the annals of the town. A public meeting was called, and it was resolved to thereafter call the town Mount Hope; by which name it has been known to the present day. The following is a copy of the act passed by the Legislature confirming the action of the citizens:

" CHAPTER 63.—AN ACT *to alter the name of the town of Calhoun. Passed March* 14, 1833.

" The people of the State of New York, represented in Senate and Assembly, do enact as follows:

" § 1. From the passage of this act, the town of Calhoun in the county of Orange, shall be known and distinguished by the name of the town of Mount Hope,"

The records of the town are very deficient in matter relating to the history of its formation, &c., the proceedings of the various town meetings previous to 1849 having been destroyed, mostly by a fire which occurred about the year 1848. The town in shape is an almost exact diamond, and embraces in its limits a large portion of the eastern slope of Shawangunk Mountain, which affords the finest scenery, it may be said, in the world, apart from our vast rivers, and which one of its citizens with just reason not long since prophesied would yet be lined with the country residences of city gentlemen. By the discovery of the valuable lead mines on Shawangunk Mountain, the resources of the town have been largely increased, and its exports are probably larger than any other town noticed in this work. The oldest landmark of the town is on the line between it and Wallkill, and is dated 1705. It has but one stream of importance—the Shawangunk kill—flowing from south to north the whole length of the town, and furnishing water power for several grist and saw mills. The name, as applied to the stream and mountain, is doubtless derived from the name of the tribe of Indians who once occupied a large share of the territory in the vicinity—the *Shanwans*, mentioned in Arent Schuyler's visit to the Minisink Region in our first chapter. The change from the word *Shanwan* to *Shawangunk*, it is obvious would be a very simple transition. The town is bounded, on the north by Sullivan county, on the west and north-west by the town of Deerpark, on the south by Minisink and Greenville, and on the east by Wallkill. The principal villages are New Vernon, in the north-eastern part; Otisville, in the western; Guymard, in the north-western; Mount Hope, in the central;

and a small collection of houses known as Finchville, in the south-west.

New Vernon is said to have been called by its present name in order to distinguish it from a place called Vernon, in New Jersey. It is a place of some business, having a store, grist mill, clover mill, woolen factory, hotel, &c.

Otisville has derived its principal source of prosperity from the construction of the Erie Railway, which crosses Shawangunk Mountain at this place; though before that event, it was a thriving little village, and done a large trade in the lumber business. It was named after Isaac Otis, who was the first merchant there, and who added greatly to its thrift. This gentleman, we believe, afterward removed to New York city. At present this village does far more business than any other in the town, having dry-goods stores, groceries, drug stores, hotels, &c.

Guymard is a flourishing village of recent origin, owing its existence to the discovery of lead a few years since on the lands of Gumaer Brothers, on the west side of Shawangunk Mountain, near the line separating the town from Deerpark. The lead was first discovered while building the road leading from the old turnpike to Gumaer's, on the canal. The largest mine, known as the Erie, is on the immediate site of the village, which is a place of almost unsurpassed rapidity of growth, now having stores, hotels, &c., some of them of large size.

Mount Hope is the oldest village in the town. It was founded by Benjamin Woodward and Dr. Benjamin B. Newkirk, on the 8th day of May, 1807. On that day they raised their dwellings on the present site of the village, and after the frames had been successfully put to their places, James Finch, Sr., in the presence of the

7*

assembled company, and with appropriate remarks, named the new village Mount Hope; a name which it still retains on this sixtieth year of its existence, and which now distinguishes the whole town. Benjamin Dodge and Stephen St. John soon after became residents of the place, and were great promoters of its prosperity. For many years it was the centre of a large trade in various commodities, especially lumber and shingles, but since the building of the Erie Railway its business has became mostly diverted to places on the line of the road. Its public buildings now comprise one church, store, hotel, &c.

OLD FAMILIES OF MOUNT HOPE.

FINCH.—This family, very illustrious in the history of the Minisink Region, is now scattered abroad, and we believe has but few if any representatives at present in the town. John Finch, the first emigrant, came from Horse Neck, Connecticut, and settled at Goshen. It is said that he was the first grown person buried in the graveyard of the Goshen church—some children having been previously buried there. His son, James Finch, Sr., was born there. He married a Miss Catherine Gale, and shortly afterward purchased the land now occupied by the site of the village of Middletown. At the time of his location there, which we judge to have been about the year 1768, there were but three log houses besides his within a mile of the place. This furnishes another example of the extraordinary growth of population so noted in some portions of Orange county. The same land is now occupied by one of the most beautiful and enterprising villages in the county. Its crowded thoroughfares, lined with splendid residences, popular places of public business, and factories whose shrill whistles vie with the hoarser scream of the locomotive, certainly form a striking contrast with the three humble log cabins in the dreary wilds where prowled the Indian, wolf and bear, scarce ninety years ago, a space of time that is frequently included in the life time of a single individual. About 1774 Mr. Finch removed to near what is now known as Finchville. His house was much resorted to for safety by fugitives from the Minisink valley during the Revolutionary war, being the nearest house to them on the east side of the mountain. Among those that came there when Brandt made his second invasion of the Minisink Region, was the wife of Major Decker, who had escaped from their home in the "lower neighborhood" in her night clothes, and led her small children by the hand, weeping as she came. The only article saved was the family bible, which she carried under her arm, and which, says Eager, in such an hour was worth more to her than Cæsar's diadem. Mr. Finch performed military duty during the old French and Indian war of 1755. He, when quite young, was waiter for Gen. Ambercrombie or some of his staff at Fort Stanwix. During the Revolutionary war he acted in the capacity of what was called a "minute man"—that is, men armed and equipped and ready for duty at a moment's warning. He was not in the battle of Minisink however, and Eager explains the reason by stating that Cols. Wisner and Phillips while marching with their men to the rendezvous, halted at Mr. Finch's to rest themselves and procure something to eat. There being nothing but salted provisions in the house, Mr. Finch killed a large fat hog for the troops. After they had eaten, the balance was placed in their knapsacks for use at some other

time, and it was resolved by them that Finch should
not go with them, but should remain at home and prepare a good meal against their return. But like the
Persian army in the old Grecian war, they were destined
never to enjoy it. Few of those who shared his hospitality on that eventful morning, ever returned to thank
him for his kindness or liberality. He died as he had
lived, an unshaken believer in the doctrines of the Baptist church, in which he had acted in the capacity of
deacon for many years.

His son, James Finch, Jr., was born July 25, 1768.
His talents brought him into public notice when quite
young. He held the office of Justice of the Peace of
Deerpark from about 1798 to 1830, excepting the time
he acted as County Judge. (Eager.) His son, Coe
Finch, succeeded him as Justice in 1831. Eager says he
held the office of Supervisor of his town twelve years
in succession, and served as member of the State Legislature thirteen sessions; but we are inclined to think it
a mistake in the latter particular, for Hough in his
" civil list," says James Finch was elected three terms,
in 1816–17 and 1833, and James Finch, Jr., six terms,
1810, '14, '15, '20, and 1824. He was married in 1794,
and had ten children : Zophar, Catherine, Margaret, P.
G., Coe, Julia, Jesse, James M., John and Sarah. He
died a firm adherent of the faith of his fathers, Dec. 7,
1843, aged seventy-five years four months and twelve
days. His public proceedings are mainly included in
the early records of the town of Deerpark, which then
included that part of the town of Mount Hope where he
resided. We believe he was the first Supervisor of the
town of Deerpark after its organization in 1798.

His family fell victims to a disease in the latter part
of the year 1843 and beginning of 1844, that proved

singularly fatal in its effects. P. G. Finch, son of James Finch, was the first attacked by it in September, 1843, and did not recover till January, 1844. This formed the basis from which the disease spread over almost the whole county, and extended somewhat into New Jersey. Mr. James Finch's wife, Sarah, and her daughter of the same name, both died the same day, December 2, 1843, and were buried in the same grave. This disease was of a bilious typhoid character, and for a long time was known and dreaded by the citizens of the surrounding country, by the name of the Finch fever; but a treatment has been found of late years that has caused it to become a comparatively mild complaint. Seven of Mr. Finch's family died with it between November 23, 1843, and February 4, 1844. D. G. Finch's house was burned in 1837–38, and with it were destroyed papers and documents of almost inestimable value in regard to the information they contained relative to the early history of the town and of the Minisink Region.

WOODWARD.—This family is among the most ancient in the town, having been closely interwoven with its history for a period of over ninety-two years. Hezekiah Woodward, Jr., and his father, Hezekiah Woodward, Sr., emigrated to this town from Stonington, Conn., in the year 1773–4, about the same time of James Finch, Sr.'s emigration to the town, and settled about a mile from where the village of Mount Hope now stands. This appears to have been the commencement of a general settlement of the vicinity, for it appears to have had quite a population of white inhabitants about 1780. Benjamin Woodward, son of Hezekiah Woodward, Jr., was born February 28, 1780. He, with Dr. Benjamin B. Newkirk, was the original founder of the village of Mount Hope, which event took place May 8, 1807, in the twenty-eighth year of his age. His talents brought him early into public notice, and he filled various offices in his town. In 1814–15, 1820–21, and 1826, he was chosen a member of the Legislature of the State, (Assembly,) and discharged the duties of his office during those years with fidelity. In 1821 he was a member of the Convention for framing the State Constitution. He was also State Senator from 1827 to 1830. His son, Charles S. Woodward, Esq., was elected Supervisor of the town for four consecutive years, commencing in 1862, and a member of the Legislature (Assembly) in 1863–64. We are indebted to this gentleman, who is a resident of Mount Hope village, for many valuable particulars relative to the early history of the town.

MILLS.—This family is undoubtedly a branch of the family of this name mentioned in Chapter XI. of this work. Isaac Mills, probably a brother of Jonathan Mills, who resided at Mills' Pond, L. I., married Sarah Phillips, a relative of the family after whom the place known as Pillipsburgh (a short distance below New Hampton, in Wawayanda,) is named. He died April 25th, 1783, aged 56 years. Ebenezer Mills, a descendant of his, was born August 3, 1759, and came from Mills' Pond to Orange county in 1787, accomplishing the journey in a sloop as far as New Windsor, and from thence to Wallkill on foot, the tour occupying sixteen days. He married Abigail Vail, of Wallkill, whose family long occupied a prominent place in the history of that town, and died February 23d, 1834. His son, Isaac Mills, Jr., was born March 5th, 1788, and married Clarissa Hulse, in 1816. They had seven children, five girls and two boys. Of these, Andrew J. Mills was born February 22d, 1821, and married Maria Green, daughter of Charles S. Green, Esq., and sister of Geo. W. Greene, Esq., of Goshen. He was a member of the Legislature (Assembly) in 1854–55. We are indebted to his kindness for valuable statistics.

GREEN.—This is a very numerous family, and we believe that at present no less than four by the name are hotel keepers in the town. They are believed to be mostly descendants of Daniel Green, who at an early period in the history of Wallkill was an extensive land owner, and the principal part of Main street in the village of Middletown is said to be built on what was part of his farm, portions of which he donated for church and educational purposes. The first who came to this section located in what is now the town of Greenville, some time during the Revolutionary war. If we are informed rightly it was the wife of Daniel Green who met with an exciting adventure with the Indians during Brandt's last invasion of the Minisink Region. Her mother was fleeing across the mountain toward Finchville, carrying her in her arms, she being a small child at the time, during the terrible scenes of that ruthless invasion. The fright and alarm had extended even to the child and she kept crying continually. At this juncture the mother spied the Indians approaching, and hid behind a log under which she held the child, expecting nothing but detection and death owing to the child's cries. But strange to relate, at this instant the child suddenly ceased crying; they were unnoticed by the savages, and escaped.

His son, Charles S. Green, Esq., married Mary Woodward, sister of Ambrose Woodward, a descendant probably of Hezekiah Woodward, of Stonington, Conn. They had ten children—six sons and four daughters.

MEMBER OF CONSTITUTIONAL CONVENTION FROM MT. HOPE.

1821   .   .   .   Benjamin Woodward.

STATE SENATOR FROM MOUNT HOPE.

1827–30 .   .   Benjamin Woodward.

MEMBERS OF ASSEMBLY FROM MOUNT HOPE.

(James Finch, Jr.'s terms of office will be found in Chapter XI.)

1814–15 ..	.	.	Benjamin Woodward.
1820–21 .	.	.	Benjamin Woodward.
1826	.	.	Benjamin Woodward.
1840	.	.	William S. Little.
1848	.	.	Augustus P. Thompson.
1854	.	.	Andrew J. Mills.
1856	.	.	Andrew J. Mills.
1862	.	.	Harvey R. Cadwell.
1863	.	.	Charles S. Woodward.
1864	.	.	Charles S. Woodward.

SCHOOL COMMISSIONER.

1866   .   .   .   B. F. Hill.

NAMES OF THE SUPERVISORS AND TOWN CLERKS OF MOUNT HOPE FROM 1849 TO THE PRESENT TIME.

SUPERVISORS.	TOWN CLERKS.
1849—Aug. P. Thompson.	John K. Seybolt.
1850—John K. Seybolt.	Ferdinand Seybolt.
1851—Wm. L. Reeve.	Lebbeus L. Harding.
1852—Wm. L. Reeve.	Lebbeus L. Harding.
1853—Wm. S. Little.	Benjamin W. Dunning.
1854—Horton Corwin.	Benjamin W. Dunning.
1855—Horton Corwin.	Lewis W. Coleman.
1856—Algernon S. Dodge.	Adam Sinsabaugh.
1857—Harvey R. Cadwell.	Ferdinand Seybolt.
1858—Harvey R. Cadwell.	Lewis A. Seybolt.

SUPERVISORS.	TOWN CLERKS.
1859—Chas. S. Woodward.	George Smith.
1860—John Mullock.	George Smith.
1861—Israel Y. Green.	George Smith.
1862—Chas. S. Woodward.	George Smith.
1863—Chas. S. Woodward.	George Smith.
1864—Chas. S. Woodward.	Reuben Frazer.
1865—Chas. S. Woodward.	Reuben Frazer.
1866—John Mullock.	James M Clinton.

Town Meeting in 1849 was held at the house of L. N. Styles, previous town records being lost.

Population in 1855, 1,735, and in 1865, 1,977—an increase of 242. Number of acres of land assessed in the town in 1865, 16,576 ; assessed value thereof, $510,450; personal property, $123,424.

CHAPTER XIII.

WAWAYANDA.—The causes which led to the formation of this town from a part of the old town of Minisink
are quite difficult to discern at the present time ; in fact
like many another change in times past, it would perhaps puzzle the originators of the scheme themselves to
account for it. It was doubtless the result of some
political party movement, since its completion has not
added materially to the welfare of the citizens of the
two towns, in a pecuniary point of view. The legislature of the State in 1848 and 1849, conferred the
power of erecting and dividing towns (previously held
by the State) on the Board of Supervisors, and the
division of Minisink was among the first that took place
under the new act. At the Town Meeting in the spring
of 1849, the following notice was given of an intention
to apply for a division of the town:

"Notice is hereby given that the undersigned freeholders of the town of Minisink, Orange county, will
make application to the Board of Supervisors at their
next annual meeting for the division of said town, to
form a new town out of that part of the town comprising the first election district."

(SIGNED)

Jacob Harding,	Usher H. Case,
David Carr,	Martin L. Mapes,
P. W. Sloat,	Isaac Denton,
J. S. Slawson,	George W. Murray,
Theophilus Dolsen,	S. Sergeant,
S. Stewart,	T. B. Denton,
Jonathan Bailey,	Alfred Wood,
Gabriel Little,	D. T. Hulse,
S. F. Gardiner,	B. F. Bailey,
R. A. Elmer,	Hiram Phillips.

The Board of Supervisors was composed as follows:

D. H. Moffat, Chairman, Blooming Grove, Whig.

Daniel Fullerton, Minisink, Whig.

Augustus P. Thompson, Mount Hope, Whig.

David Swartout, Deerpark, Whig.

William V. N. Armstrong, Warwick, Whig.

Morgan Shuit, Monroe, Whig.

Odell S. Hathaway, Newburgh, Whig.

William Jackson, Hamptonburgh, Whig.

Lindley M. Ferris, Montgomery, Whig.

Hezekiah Moffat, Chester, Whig.

Augustus Thompson, Crawford, Democrat.

Richard M. Vail, Goshen, Democrat.

Abraham Vail, Jr., Wallkill, Democrat.

James Denniston, Cornwall, Democrat.

James R. Dickson, New Windsor, Democrat.

On the 27th day of November (1849) the matter was brought before the Board on motion of Mr. Fullerton of Minisink, the petitioner for the division, the maps and survey of the proposed new town, made by Dr. D. C. Hallock, having been previously presented by him. He then proposed to name the town "Wawayanda," after the old Indian patent upon which it is located; the name being an Indian word, used by an Indian while standing on a hill, defining the boundaries of the tract to the early settlers, and supposed to mean "way over yonder."

Mr. Fullerton then moved the passage of the bill, which was seconded by Mr. Ferris, when the house was called by towns and voted as follows:

Ayes—D. H. Moffat, Hezekiah Moffat, Lindley M. Ferris, Daniel Fullerton, Wm. V. N. Armstrong, A. P. Thompson, David Swartout, William Jackson, Odell. S. Hathaway, Morgan Shuit.

Nays—R. M. Vail, Abraham Vail, Jr., James Denniston, James R. Dickson, Augustus Thompson.

It was therefore declared carried.

The town is bounded on the east by the town of Goshen, south by Warwick and Minisink, west by Greenville, and north by Mount Hope and Wallkill. Rutger's creek forms part of the boundary line on the south, and the Wallkill on the east and south-east.

The principal villages are, Hampton on the Erie Railway, Ridgebury and Brookfield in the central part of the town, Gardnersville in the southern, and Millsburgh and Centreville in the south-western portion.

Hampton is a small village owing its importance to the fact that it is the only station in the town on the railroad. Its public buildings consist of a hotel, three stores, tin shop, &c. There are grist mills a short distance below, at Phillipsburg, on the Wallkill; also a hotel and store about half a mile south, at Denton.

Ridgebury is said to have taken its name from the Presbyterian church first erected at that place, which was so called from the number of berries that grew on a neighboring ridge, still known as " whortleberry hill." It is an old established place, and the site of the village was owned in 1800 by Benjamin Dunning, Jonathan Bailey, Benjamin Howell, Isaac Decker and others. John Dunken, killed at the battle of Minisink, was from this locality. John Hallock, Sr., James Hulse, Benj. Smith, Moses Overton, Noyes Wickham, Richard Ellison and Charles Durland, were early settlers in the neighborhood. The business part of the village at present is a hotel and store.

Brookfield is undoubtedly named from its proximity to a brook, which nearly surrounds it. It was early settled, and before the construction of the Erie Railway was a place of some notoriety, having a printing office, grist mill, plaster mill, saw mill, tannery, &c. At present it has but one hotel and store.

Gardnersville is named after Ira Gardner, who formerly owned the mills and kept store at the place. It is situated on Rutger's kill, and has a grist mill, saw mill and one or two stores.

Millsburgh and Centreville are but a short distance apart, both situated on the outlet of the Binnewater pond. Millsburgh was formerly called Racine, after Mr. John Racine, who resided there. It is also known with Centreville as Wells' Corners. Two grist mills, two saw mills and two stores make up the business portion of the two places.

OLD FAMILIES OF WAWAYANDA.

HALLOCK.—The ancestor of this family, John Hallock, Sr., came from England before the Revolutionary war, and settled at Mattatuck, Long Island. At the commencement of the war he was doing military duty on

the Island, and left it when it was captured by the
English. He then removed to Oxford, in Orange
county, and was in the military service some time in
the Highlands. His brother Daniel was acting as his
substitute at the capture of Fort Montgomery in 1777,
and narrowly escaped being taken prisoner. In 1783
he purchased two hundred acres of land of John Scott,
just south of the present village of Ridgebury. The
land extended west and included the site of the village
of Brookfield. He gave the lot upon which the Old
School Baptist church stands in that place. Eager says
(page 416) that when he was building his log cabin he
fell short of nails, and in order to raise funds, traded off
a good new hat for one of less value, and purchased the
nails with the difference. His son, John Hallock, Jr.,
was a man of ability, and very quick witted, with a fund
of perpetual good humor. These qualities brought him
before the public, and he was elected to offices of
various grades in the old town of Minisink (before its
division)—Justice of the Peace, Town Clerk, and a
number of terms as Supervisor, all of which duties he
discharged with energy and integrity. He was afterward elected twice a member of the State Legislature,
also a member of the 19th and 20th Congresses.
His former residence is now owned by Mr. Randall
Stivers, of Ridgebury. His son, Dr. Dewitt C. Hallock,
inherited a large share of his father's talents. He held
two or three terms as Town Clerk of Minisink, and after
the town of Wawayanda was set off, was elected Supervisor of the new town in 1852 and 1853. He was said
to be a good surveyor, had an extensive practice as a
physician, and was noted for his extraordinary powers
as a violinist, in which he was said to excel any player
in the State.

DOLSEN.—This family is said to be of Dutch origin. Eager says (p. 412) that there is a family tradition to the effect that the first male child born in New Amsterdam (now New York) was a Dolsen. The first of the name in this town was Isaac Dolsen, who came from Fishkill, in Duchess county, in 1756, and purchased seven hundred acres in what is now known as Dolsentown. He was a millwright by trade, and married Polly Huzzy of New Jersey. He died in 1795, leaving two children, James and Isaac. Isaac was never married. James married Phebe Meeker, and their children were James, Asa, Samuel, Polly and Abby. The Indians committed some depredations near Dolsentown in the French and Indian war. The wife of David Cooley, whose farm joined Dolsen's, was shot by the Indians between the oven and house, and tradition says that her blood, which bespattered the stones, remained there for years, resisting all efforts of the rain to wash it out. The scene of this tragedy is now owned by the heirs of Capt. John Cummings.

DAVIS.—The original settler in this vicinity by that name was Joshua Davis, Sr., who settled on the farm now owned by Col. William C. Carpenter, about a mile and a-half south of Brookfield, some time previous to the year 1780. He built the stone dwelling-house on this farm about 1787, which would make it at the present time seventy-nine years old. It is still standing in good condition—a monument of the stability of old-time workmanship—and likely to remain so for years to come. Mr. Davis was the driver of the first vehicle on wheels that ever passed over the road from Goshen through Ridgebury. This was a rude two wheeled ox-cart, and no doubt was considered a great innovation by the few settlers in these parts, the road being then a mere path. He left four daughters and two sons—Joshua and James. Joshua married a daughter of Noah Terry, Esq., and James, a Mrs. Decker whose husband went to Nova Scotia after the conclusion of the Revolution. The only one of the daughters married, married Richard Ferguson, Esq., whose father was an early settler in this section and built the mills at Gardnersville now owned by C. W. Fowler, Esq. By this marriage they had eight children—five daughters and three sons. One daughter married George Jackson, Esq., and their descendants generally reside in the town. One married Charles Reeve, Esq., of Newburgh, one —— Ellison, Esq., and one —— Hoyle, Esq., whose descendants mostly reside in the State of Ohio.

Lawrence Ferguson, Esq., married a daughter of Charles Durland, and at present resides in the town of Minisink. (For many of the above items relating to this family we are indebted to Miss Julia Ferguson, of Newburgh.)

Joseph Davis, Esq., late President of the Middletown Bank, formerly Assemblyman from this district, and Supervisor of this town for several years, if we are informed correctly, is of another family. He married a daughter of —— Decker, Esq., of Minisink. The male line of his family became extinct a few months since by the death of his only son, Henry E. Davis, Esq.

DENTON.—Rev. Richard Denton was the first ancestor, and came to Boston, Massachusetts, with Gov. Winthrop, in the year 1630. He preached in Watertown, Mass., and afterwards at Weathersfield and Stamford, Conn., until 1644, when he emigrated with a number of his congregation and commenced the settlement of Hempstead, Long Island. He was a graduate of Cambridge, England, and settled as minister of Coley Chapel, Halitax, before coming to America. He returned to England and died there in 1662, aged seventy-six years. He left five sons—Richard, Samuel, Daniel, Nathaniel and John. John removed to Orange county. James, his son, had four sons—Amos, Thomas, William and John. The last named located on what was called the old Carpenter farm in Goshen. He had three wives and fourteen children. His first wife was Jane Fisher, of Long Island; his second, Elizabeth Wisner, daughter of Henry Wisner, Esq., of Wallkill; and his third, Mary Gale, daughter of Hezekiah Gale, who lived near what is now called Lagrange. One of his daughters married Jason Wilkin, of the last named place. Before what is now known as the village of Denton came into the possession of the Denton family, Thaddeus B. and Henry W. Denton, it was called the Outlet. Elisha Eldridge, from New England, built a store and tavern there (the first) about the commencement of the Revolution. Previous to that time it was owned by Richard Carpenter. It is now mostly owned by Theodore J. Denton, and Reuben C. Mead, who married a sister of Theodore's. At present they are probably among the wealthiest citizens of the town.

HOWELL.—In 1800 an early settler by the name of Benjamin Howell resided near Ridgebury, but we believe that at present none of his descendants are living in the town. John Howell, a brother of his, must have moved to this town at about the year 1778. He was an old sailor—had been on one or two whaling voyages to the Arctic Regions, besides numerous trips to other shores "before the mast" of a merchantman. He also served as a soldier in the Continental army during the war of the Revolution. He was in the battle of Minisink, 1779, and among the few that escaped.

8

Before coming to this town he had resided at what is known as Sugar Loaf, in the town of Warwick. He died in 1790, leaving six children, and was buried at the corners, about two miles below Ridgebury, where for years his grave, solitary and alone among the bushes, was a sort of sacred spot to the passer by. Since then others of his connection have gone to their long rest near him, and the whole, ornamented with tasteful monuments and enclosed with a substantial iron fence, now forms one of the most beautiful cemeteries in the town.

One of his daughters married Reuben Cash, another John Roberts, another Eliphalet Stickney, and one, Hepsibah, remained unmarried. The homestead was kept by his two sons, John and Jeffrey. Jeffrey married a daughter of Peter Corwin, Esq., and had seven children ; but by a strange fatality, all died with the consumption before attaining the age of thirty-two years. Jeffrey died in 1837.

John Howell, Jr., married the widow of Moses Knapp, and sister of Alanson Kimball, Esq., but she was accidentally drowned, while crossing the outlet of Binnewater pond, near Pine Ridge, in search of herbs for some medicinal purpose, June 24th, 1834 ; having been married scarce a year. The male line of this family has become extinct with the death of this last survivor of the family.

CASH.—This family has also become extinct, by the death of James M. Cash, Jr. Reuben. Cash, the first mentioned in old annals, was a survivor of the Wyoming Massacre, 1778. He escaped with his mother, and she led him by the hand through the wilderness to Minisink, he being a small boy at the time. He married a daughter of John Howell, Sr., and had nine children. One of

his daughters married Roswell Mead, another married
Samuel Vail, Sr., another married John E. S. Gardner,
and another married Parmenas Horton. Merit H. Cash
kept the old homestead. He married a daughter of
Joseph Davis, Esq., but had no children. James M.
Cash, Sr., married a daughter of —— White, Esq., by
whom he had one son, who died young, and in whom
the name of Cash became extinct as first mentioned.
John Morris Cash married a daughter of Ira Gardner,
Esq. Solomon V. R. Cash married a daughter of
Joseph Davis, Esq. Selah Cash died quite young, and
was never married.

Merit H. adopted the profession of a physician, and
became quite a successful one. He held various civil
offices in the old town of Minisink before its division,
and was elected three times a member of the New
York Legislature.

STICKNEY.—William Stickney, the first of the name of
whom we have any knowledge, settled at Rowley, Massachusetts, in 1639. One of the name held a colonel's
commission in the Revolutionary war, and was at the
battle of Bennington under Gen. Stark, as mentioned in
Eastman's History of New York (page 230). Eliphalet
Stickney, son of Dr. James Stickney, of Newburgh, was
the earliest resident of this vicinity, and married a
daughter of John Howell, Sr. They had eight children,
Erastus, Charles, John, Benjamin, William, Julia, Harriet
and Charlotte. The family afterwards removed west,
except Erastus and Julia. Erastus married a daughter
of Prentice Allyn, Esq., of Sullivan county. He was
elected to various civil offices in the town of Minisink
before its division, and was elected a member of the
New York legislature from Wawayanda in 1857.

MEAD.—Roswell Mead removed to this town, we believe, from New England. He purchased the farm near Brookfield (previously owned by Festus A. Webb, who bought it of Richard Wood, father of Oliver E. and Lewis C. Wood,) now owned by William H. Wood. He married a daughter of Reuben Cash, by whom he had six children. He was elected Supervisor, and held various offices in the town of Minisink, and was also elected a member of the New York legislature in 1842. His sons William H. and Reuben C., still reside in the town. William married a daughter of Joseph Davis, and Reuben, a daughter of Theodorus Denton.

DURLAND.—Charles Durland, the first resident of the town of this name, emigrated to the town some time previous to the year 1800. He first settled near Bushville, in the present town of Greenville, when the whole vicinity was a dense forest, and the only road from there to Ridgebury was a narrow path among the brush. He moved from there to near Ridgebury, and for a time kept a public house on the premises now owned by Gilbert H. Budd. In 1800 he resided on the farm now owned by his son, Thomas T. Durland. Daniel and Stewart T. Durland, of Greenville, and Addison Durland, of Minisink, are also sons of his. The family is reputed to be very ancient, and of unswerving fidelity to the cause of Independence during Revolutionary times.

HOLBERT.—Peter Holbert, Sr., is the first mentioned in old records. He was elected a member of the New York legislature in 1812, Supervisor of the town of Minisink in 1813, and Town Clerk for one or two terms. His son, Peter Holbert, Jr., married a daughter of Wm. Robertson, and sister of James F. Robertson.

TOOKER.—We are not informed of the exact date the pioneers of this family first came to the town. Samuel Tooker, surveyor, married Catherine, daughter of James

Finch, Sr., of Mount Hope, and is the first we have any knowledge of. His son, Charles Tooker, settled near Brookfield, and left two sons, James H. and Samuel S. Tooker. His daughter Julia married James F. Vail, who at present resides on the old homestead near Brookfield. Henry Tucker was elected Town Clerk of Minisink in 1791 and 1792, and Supervisor from 1799 to 1807; but as the name is spelled differently, we presume him to have been of another family.

REED.—This is an old established family, of the exact date of whose settlement in the town we are not informed. Samuel Reed, Sr., (his father being the original settler,) died but a few years ago, at a very advanced age. His widow died a few months since, and though a very aged lady, was possessed of a remarkable memory. She distinctly recollected seeing the people go to the Minisink battle in 1779. Three of her neighbors met under an apple tree for that purpose, near her father's house, and though very small at the time, she remembered the parting scene plainly. Two of them perished in the battle, we believe. Daniel Reed was killed in the battle; whether a relative or not is not known.

WICKHAM.—This family is quite numerous in the town, and are believed to be mostly descendants of Noyes Wickham, who lived near Ridgebury in 1800.

REEVE.—The first of the name mentioned in old records is James Reeve, who escaped from the battle of Minisink with a broken arm. Two of his sons, James M. and John H., still reside in the town. John H. Reeve was elected Supervisor of Wawayanda from 1861 to 1866.

MEMBER OF ASSEMBLY FROM WAWAYANDA.

1857 . . . . : Erastus Stickney.

NAMES OF SUPERVISORS AND TOWN CLERKS OF WAWAYANDA
FROM ITS ORGANIZATION IN 1849 TO 1866.

SUPERVISORS.	TOWN CLERKS.
1850—Daniel Fullerton.	Holloway W. Stephens.
1851—Daniel Fullerton.	Oliver Lewis.
1852—Dewitt C. Hallock.	Oliver Lewis.
1853—Dewitt C. Hallock.	Oliver Lewis.
1854—Joseph Davis.	Oliver Lewis.
1855—Joseph Davis.	James F. Robertson.
1856—Gideon W. Cock.	Wilmot C. Terry.
1857—Joseph Davis.	Wilmot C. Terry.
1858—Joseph Davis.	Mathew H. Bailey.
1859—Joseph Davis.	John M. Howell.
1860—Joseph Davis.	John M. Howell.
1861—John H. Reeve.	James L. Mills.
1862—John H. Reeve.	John M. Howell.
1863—John H. Reeve.	John M. Howell.
1864—John H. Reeve.	Oliver Lewis.
1865—John H. Reeve.	William H. Wood.
1866—John H. Reeve.	Charles E. Stickney.

The first town meeting was held at D. C. Hallock's, Brookfield.

Population in 1855, 2,069; and in 1865, 1,906—a decrease of 163.

Number of acres of land assessed in 1865, 19,677; assessed value, $706,250; personal property, $100,770.

TOWN OF GREENVILLE.

The records of this town are somewhat deficient in regard to its early formation. The census of 1855 dates its organization in 1850; but we are inclined to consider it an error, because the first town meeting in the new town is shown by the records to have been held in 1854.

The town being erected by the Board of Supervisors, it was most probably done at their annual meeting in the fall of the previous year (Dec. 3, 1853.) At that time the Board of Supervisors was composed of the following gentlemen, viz.:

Albert A. Seymour,	. .	Minisink.
Dewitt C. Hallock,	. .	Wawayanda.
Samuel J. Farnum,	. .	Newburgh.
Morgan Shuit,	. .	Monroe.
Henry C. Seeley,	. .	Warwick.
Calvin Gardner,	. .	Goshen.
J. H. McLaughlin,	. .	Blooming Grove.
Stephen Rapelje,	. .	Montgomery.
Vincent Booth,	. .	Hamptonburgh.
John Denniston,	. .	Cornwall.
Edward L. Norris,	. .	Warwick.
William S. Little,	. .	Mount Hope.
—— ——	. .	Deerpark.
Halstead Sweet,	. .	Wallkill.

The motives that prompted its formation, and the prime movers of it, are alike unknown to us. It was formed from Minisink, Mount Hope and Deerpark; and in 1855 had a population of 1,218; and in 1865, 1,147— a decrease of 41. We are ignorant of the origin of its name, but presume it was named Greenville from its situation—lying as it does mostly along the sunny slopes of the eastern side of Shawangunk Mountain, the fields of which are covered with green verdure the earliest in the year. The name was first applied to a small village near the foot of the mountain; afterwards used in giving a name to the new town. It is bounded on the north by Mount Hope and Deerpark, on the east by Minisink and Wawayanda, on the south by the State of New Jersey, and on the west by Deerpark. Its principal streams are Indigot creek, the source of Rutger's creek, Binnewater pond and its outlet, and the source of Shawangunk kill.

The principal village of the town is Greenville, situated in the central part, on the road leading from Goshen to Carpenter's Point. The road crosses the Shawangunk, the northwest boundary of the town, at this place. For some time after its first settlement it was called Minisink village. At present it consists of a hotel, store, two churches, &c. Bushville and Centre Point are small villages, but at present no business is carried on in them of any importance.

We are not possessed of much information in regard to the old families of the town. The section of country it includes was undoubtedly not settled as early as some of the more favored localities. For this reason probably its population is mostly made up of the descendants of old established families in adjoining towns. Timothy Wood, probably one of the earliest settlers, was a signer of the Revolutionary pledge in 1775, and his name is mentioned as holding various offices in the early history of the town of Minisink. Arthur Van Tuyle was a signer of the pledge of 1775, and after the organization of the town of Minisink the first town meeting was held at his house, April, 1789. Jacob Quick, Solomon Cuykendall, Moses Cortright, Peter Cole and others, who signed the pledge, were probably from this section.

SCHOOL COMMISSIONER FROM GREENVILLE.

1859 . . . Harvey H. Clark.

JUSTICES OF SESSIONS FROM GREENVILLE.

1862 . . . Stewart T. Durland.
1863 . . . Stewart T. Durland.
1864 . . . Stewart T. Durland.
1865 . . . Stewart T. Durland.

NAMES OF SUPERVISORS AND TOWN CLERKS OF GREENVILLE FROM ITS ORGANIZATION IN 1853 TO 1866.

SUPERVISORS.	TOWN CLERKS.
1854—Timothy Wood.	Isaac Winters.
1855—Timothy Wood.	Harvey H. Clark.
1856—Isaac M. Seybolt.	W. L. Clark.
1857—Isaac M. Seybolt.	Alfred L. Clark.
1858—Isaac M. Seybolt.	Leonard Bell, Jr.
1859—Jesse V. Myers.	Harvey H. Clark.
1860—Isaac M. Seybolt.	Harvey H. Clark.
1861—Jesse V. Myers.	Stoddard W. Slawson.
1862—Stewart T. Durland.	Albert Shute.
1863—Stewart T. Durland.	Albert Shute.
1864—Isaac M. Seybolt.	Ezra T. Durland.
1865—Harvey H. Clark.	William B. Jenks.
1866—Harvey H. Clark.	Samuel W. Reed.

First town meeting was held at the house of Jonathan Wood, Bushville, 1854.

Number of acres of land assessed in 1865—18,287; assessed value, $385,600; personal property, $49,850.

8*

CHAPTER XIV.

A venerable old building was the "Old Greycourt," as the old inn was known in those days of troublous times that marked the period of the Revolutionary struggle.

Situated on the main road leading from New Jersey to the eastern part of Orange county, on the edge of the low, rich, flat meadow lands that extend into·the township of Chester ; and owning for its proprietor an old pioneer of the country, Daniel Cromline, who had founded it in 1716, it could not fail of being popular. Many a jovial revel had the old house seen in those wild stormy days of Indian warfare ; and many a trying time too, since the stout hearts that beat obedience to Washington had ranged themselves against the troopers of old King George. Many a dark redskin had the old goose, that was painted as large as life on the swinging sign, seen pass beneath her shadow for a drink of the fire-water, and many a true patriot had she seen pledge a comrade with undying friendship in a last glass at the familiar bar, before departing for the army ; where, perhaps, some Hessian bullet had quickly closed his career. The old goose, too, had a history, for it was said to have supplied a name for the inn. When the house was first built, it became necessary, according to custom, to place above the door the arms of royalty; and the proprietor, in doing so, had the picture of the white goose placed beside it, because of its proximity to Goose Pond Lake. At first almost a thing of life, it fairly threatened to take wing and join its wild kindred of the wilderness; but, alas, the colors only seemed to vanish with the sun, rain, and storm of years, until at last, wondrously grey, and with a countenance marvelously weather-beaten, the antique old goose looked down upon the throng of customers that still passed beneath her wing. The rebellion against the authority of England caused the sign to become the butt of endless jokes and gibes by the patriotic. Not at the old goose, for she was too national a bird to be sneered at, but at the coat of arms by her side, which, for a time, was called "Grey Coat," and then changed to "Grey Court," by which appellation the house became known far and wide. The building was constructed for durability; and that it met the end aimed at may be known by the fact that it stood for a space of one hundred and sixteen years. But it has now passed away, in common with the hearts that planned, and the hands that built it. The man that stood behind the bar, the man that stood upon the other side, the lounger that hung around its hall all the day long, and the young man who affected the beau, wore his hat so jauntily, and talked and laughed with the pretty maids of all work, have all gone to the silence of oblivion. Their little likes and dislikes, that so agitated their bosoms; their hopes, fears, troubles and disappointments; the good they have done, and the bad, might as well have been buried with their bones, for all that is known, felt, or cared for now.

A goodly company is assembled in the bar-room as we glance into it this pleasant evening, away back through the years that have flown since November of the year 1778. They are not talking of the war, though the liberty of America is being chipped from the granite power of England daily. No — something of new interest engages them.

"So they have got him safe at last," said a plethoric, middle-aged man, in a drab coat and lapstone hat.

" Yes," replied an old man, in a kind of voice like a person just rescued from some great danger, "and I'm glad of it; folks can sleep now of nights, and not be afraid of getting their throats cut before morning by Claudius Smith."

"He ain't going to stretch hemp a bit too soon for the good of society," observed a third.

"Yet he had some good qualities about him, in spite of what people say," commenced a cleanly looking old man, as he took a pinch of snuff from a ponderous box of the kind, the lid of which was shut with an experienced tap. "You remember Col. McClaughry, that was taken prisoner by the British at the capture of Fort Montgomery, in October of last year. Well, they took him to New York and locked him up with the rest, and, it seems, didn't treat him very well. So they gave him leave to write home for some things he wanted, or some money to get them with. His wife hadn't got any, so she went over to Abimal Youngs' to borrow some; but Abimal said he had none, though every one knew he was as rich as a Jew. It was a pretty tough case — her husband starving in that cursed prison-house, and she not able to get him anything. It made quite a talk, and everybody who knew her felt sorry for her ; but that didn't help the matter. She sold her shoe-buckles and other ornaments, but that didn't go a great way. By and by it came to Claudius Smith's ears, and one night he went to old Abimal's house, determined to get the money for her. His men took Abimal out of doors, and threatened to hang him if he didn't tell where his money was. He wouldn't, so they put a rope round his neck, tied it to the well-pole, and slung him up. After he had hung a moment, they let him down, and again demanded his money, knowing he had some somewhere. But he still refused, clinging to his money in preference to his life, so they again hung him up. However, they could'nt make him tell, so at last they let him go. Determined to inflict some loss, they carried off his deeds, mortgages, &c., and he never got them again."

"And served him right," said the man with the lap-stone hat. "But I always heard that his father was always called a bad kind of man around Brookhaven, on Long Island, where Claudius was born. And still more so after he moved to McKnight's Mills, down by Smith's Clove, as it was called—a little west of the highlands in the Ramapo valley. Once, when the old man was returning home from the mountains, where he had been to carry some provisions to Claudius and his gang of tories who were secreted there, the scouts who were watching for them, espied him and fired at him. The horse he rode was killed, but he escaped. Before he died, too, they say he got mightily cross and ill-willed; and after he got so, he could not move without his cane, would strike with it at everybody that came near him; and was known to follow his wife around the room for the purpose of hitting her with it. Ah, it was in the breed for them to be rogues. When Claudius was a boy, he was such a vicious, ugly fellow, that his mother said to him :

" 'Claudius, you will die like a trooper's horse, with your shoes on.' "

"He was a cursed Tory besides, and no longer than last year, he was in Goshen jail for stealing beef cattle from the government. They thought he would be safer in Kingston jail, but while moving him, he got away. But he won't get away now, I guess ; they keep him manacled and heavily chained, and have parties guarding him night and day, with instructions to shoot him if a rescue is attempted, or if he tries to escape."

"Oh, he'll swing for it now, no doubt," said the snuff-taker, again resorting to his box for a fresh pinch. "But then he has some good traits, as I said before. For instance, there is Major Bodle's adventure. About the time of the capture of Fort Montgomery, he was making his way from that place towards home, when, in the morning, he met Claudius Smith, hailed him with a friendly good-morning, calling him by name, and shaking hands with him. After inquiring as to the news from the fort, &c., he continued—

" 'Mr. Bodle, you are weary with walking, go to my house yonder (pointing to a place off the road) and tell my wife to get you some breakfast. Tell her I sent you.' "

"The Major made believe to accept the offer, and thanked him with much kindness ; but as soon as he was out of sight, he struck a bee-line for home, and hardly paused to look around till he had almost reached there."

"Perhaps," said the man with the timid voice, who had indulged in a bit of a snooze, and just aroused himself in time to hear the Major's adventure, "perhaps he was only trying to get him off the main road, while he robbed him. I wouldn't have trusted him either; only think how he served Col. Jesse Woodhull. The Col. never harmed him or any of his men, yet he swore he would kill him, Nathaniel Strong, Cole Curtis and Samuel Strong. Then after all, when the Colonel saved his life by not shooting him when he had a chance, see how the ungrateful fellow used him. The Colonel did not dare sleep in his own house for months, for fear of his fulfilling the threat. He then threatened to steal a mare the Colonel thought a great deal of. In order to save her, the Colonel had her brought into the cellar of his house, yet this same Claudius Smith you're praising so, lurking devil that he was, watched his opportunity, and when the Colonel and his family were at tea, boldly slipped the mare from the cellar, though in broad daylight, and the first intimation the unconscious inmates had of their nearness to danger was the yell of defiance given by the highwayman as he rode off his stolen prize. A gentleman present at the table sprang to his rifle, and as the robber was still in easy range, leveled it at him, but Woodhull knocked aside his arm, so great was his fear of the rascal, saying, 'For heaven's sake, don't fire; if you miss him, he will kill me.' Not yet content, this merciless Tory came to his house again on the night of October 6th, only last month, for the purpose of robbing and murdering the Colonel and his family, for nothing in particular, only because Woodhull was such a 'darned rebel,' as he said. Their intended victim was fortunately away, doing duty in the American army, as he is now. The Colonel's wife, hearing them coming, hid her silver ware and other articles of value in the cradle, and placed her child upon them. When the gang broke open the door, and all the time they

were searching the house, she busied herself in trying
to keep her child still. It deceived them and saved
her goods. They did not get a great deal of plunder.
The child was quite a bit of a girl, large enough to talk,
and she asked her mother if they were going to steal
her calico dress. They stole the horse of Luther Conklin, who had been staying at the Colonel's, and went off.
The same night, they went to Major Nathaniel Strong's
house about 12 o'clock, when they were all asleep, and
broke in the outside door, and a panel out of the inner
door, connecting with the Major's bedroom. This
alarmed the Major, who came out of his room armed
with his pistols and gun. As soon as he entered the
inside room, he was fired at through the window, but
was not hit. His assailants then promised that if he
would give up his arms, they would not harm him. As
he was in their power, and could do but little less, he
resolved to rely upon their promises, and accordingly
put down his gun, and advanced towards the door as if
to open it. But their hearts were callous to broken
promises and the influence of mercy. Ere he had
reached it, they fired through the broken panel, and he
expired without speaking a word—pierced through the
heart by two of the faithless Tory's bullets. Leaving
the murdered corpse with the terror-stricken family,
they decamped, taking with them his saddle and bridle.
And yet, some men will contend that they had good
traits in their characters. A fig for such talk, I say,"
and the voice that had become really eloquent with
earnestness again lowered to its old timid tone, and the
speaker sank back in his chair, as if having said his say,
he was ready for another snooze.

During the latter part of the narration of these incidents, which, being familiar to all, they knew to be true,

the snuff-taker had waxed uneasy, and began to snuff
with increased vehemence; and on its conclusion, he
broke out with—

"I didn't praise Claudius Smith; I said he had some
good points about his disposition, and I've always heard
it said that much of that he stole from the rich he gave
to the poor. I say he has a humane heart, and I can
back up my opinion too, call me a tory or what you
will."

"It must have been a mighty small one, since so few
people ever found it out," said he of the timid voice.

"Never mind, gentlemen," said the landlord, laugh-
ing, "you needn't either one get your back up about
your opinions. They are good enough without any
backing. If you'll just keep still a little while, I'll tell
you a story about Edward Roblin, one of the most noted
of Claudius' gang; in fact his right hand man. They
say he knows where all the caves and secret retreats
are in Smith's Clove and along the Ramapo, and where
he has buried the gold and silver he has stolen. Well,
I've been told that when a boy, none was thought more
honest or better behaved than he. And the way he
got to be a freebooter and tory was a little romantic, to
say the least. He worked down toward the river from
here, for an old man by the name of Price. A mere
boy when he first came there, he proved such a hard-
working, steady, trustworthy little fellow, that the old
farmer was glad to keep him on, and so he staid, and
worked, and delved, till he grew at last to be a tall
handsome lad, and all the girls cast sidelong glances at
him in church, and felt pleased when he spoke or nod-
ded to them, and thought how proud they would be if
some good looking manly form, like this, should stand
beside them some pleasant evening, and put a tiny ring

upon their finger before the priest, thereby sealing both
in bonds for life. Now this employer had an only
daughter who had grown up to womanhood at the same
time as himself, being about the same age. Beautiful
when a child, she lost none of her sweetness with her
years, but seemed rather to increase in angelic purity
and loveliness. Her form and features were among the
most perfect works of nature, and when she added to it
those many little artificial attractions that females know
so well how to use, and the blandishment of a clear
silvery voice, all attuned to melody and love—woe, woe
to the susceptible heart, of lord or peasant, that
rendered itself liable to this grand combination of
charms. This young couple did not fall in love with
each other, for that was impossible; since they had
loved when children, and it had been strengthening
with their growth, year by year. But young Roblin
was poor; and when he at last spoke to old Price about
marriage, it resulted just as he expected. The old man
locked his weeping daughter in her bedroom up stairs,
and forbade her ever speaking to the young man again.
But he didn't discharge Roblin, and the result was just
what he might have expected, but didn't. One morning he rose early, and as was usual called to Roblin,
but no Roblin answered; so after a little while he
opened the bedroom door, but no Roblin was there, and
the bed bore the appearance of having been slept in
but about half the night. He at once mistrusted the
cause, and at the instant started for his daughter's
room. Her bed bore the same appearance; and the
open window, and, when the old farmer looked out of it
the sight of his long ladder reaching from the ground to
the casement, its rounds wet with dew and sparkling in
the early morning light, at once explained the mystery.

He hurried down stairs and out to his stables, but Roblin had been too honest for his own safety—the horses
were there. 'Forgad,' quoth old Price, 'I'll have them
yet; for,' thought he, 'they've gone to the minister's on
foot, and that's some miles,—they won't get there much
before noon, and,' cried the old fellow chuckling, 'by
that time I'll be there, too.'

"He lost no time in mounting on horseback, and was
off for the Squire's in a twinkling. Here he procured a
warrant for Roblin's arrest for debt, on account of some
money he had advanced him, in reality for work done.
He next found the constable, and placing the document
in his hands the two worthies sped off for the dominie's.
He didn't arrive there a whit too soon, for Roblin and
his bride had just taken their places before the good man
as they burst into the room.

"'Ha! ha! my pretty birds, I've caught you, have I,'
yelled the old man as he grasped his daughter's arm.
'You thought to catch a weasel asleep, did you?'

"At first Roblin thought of resistance, but he dare not
resist the authority of the law; so he gave his betrothed
a farewell kiss, and quietly submitting was soon on his
way to a cell in Goshen jail, and his mourning sweet
one traveling sorrowfully homeward with her cruel
father. The law, you know, is unusually severe for the
nonpayment of debt, so Roblin lay in limbo, month in
and month out, with no signs of release. He procured
a violin, was soon a good player, and in that amusement
passed much of his time. On the still pleasant evenings,
crowds of the young people of the village would gather
underneath his window, to listen to the varied airs of
delicious melody that floated on the clear air from out
the bars of his grated cell. And as the slippered
feet of the fair village maids kept time to the measured

cadence of the music, their eyes often glanced up toward its source, anxious to catch a glimpse of the handsome sad face of the player, the story of whose disappointment in love they all knew. His betrothed, unable to withstand the constant commands and urgings of her tyrant father, at last yielded to his solicitations, and married the man he chose; though it was a current saying of the old dames in the neighborhood, that he had taken her from her betters, and given her to her inferiors. When the news was taken to young Roblin, in prison, you may be sure he felt bad enough; and it was a long time before the music of his violin was heard outside the grated walls. Even when it was again heard, its strains were so melancholy and touching, so expressive of a sorrowful heart, that many a maiden's heart beat with sympathy for the imprisoned lover. The pretty daughter of the jail-keeper, when she took the dinner to the prisoners, always handed in the fullest plate at the door of his cell, and the jailor himself, when he went his rounds at night, spoke a kind word through the grate of the door in passing by. Interest began to be taken by influential citizens toward procuring his discharge, and everybody was anxious to have something done for him. But he did not wait their kind offices. One morning the jailor espied the door of the jail wide open, and on entering found the cell of Roblin empty. He had evidently escaped by the help of some outsider. An inspection of his own dwelling revealed the cause of his escape, and also the fact, that his demure daughter who had taken such an interest in the prisoner, had no doubt become herself the prisoner of love, and flown with her lover to the realms of bliss. But what was still worse, when her father visited his stables, he found that Roblin had not forgotten the horse this time, for the stall of his beautiful chestnut gelding was empty, with the exception of a limb from the chestnut tree in the yard, which was tied to the manger with this inscription, in large letters on an old paper:

'MY DEAR FATHER-IN-LAW—As you will be when you see this, pardon the liberty I have taken in exchanging horses with you, though you must conclude yourself there was no great difference ; I acknowledge this is a horse of another color, still as yours was a chestnut horse, the exchange is fair, for this is a horse chestnut. It's the best legacy I can leave you at present, coupled with the best wishes of   EDWARD ROBLIN.'

"The jailor took it quite hard for a time, but people said he grieved more for the loss of his steed than his daughter; since, as soon as she disappeared, all the village dames suddenly discovered her to have been a conceited, shiftless minx, and fit for nobody but a scapegrace like Roblin. Nothing was heard of him for a long time after, till at last he suddenly appeared among the band of outlaws headed by "The Scourge of the Highlands," and by his daring villainies soon won a reputation second only to his chief. The man that wedded old Price's daughter turned out to be a poor miserable fellow, and soon abandoned her and was never heard of more. Disappointed, cruelly forsaken, and heart sick, she returned to her father's house. The doctors could do nothing to relieve her depression of spirits, and she rapidly went into a decline, lingered awhile and died, the neighbors said, of a broken heart."   *   *

For a moment after the conclusion of the story, the utmost silence was observed. Its simple details awoke a more than ordinary feeling in the rough breasts of the auditors. The snuff taker, who had become so interested

in the narrative as to forget the pinch he held idly between his thumb and finger, was the first to break the
pause:

" A curious story, truly. Edward Roblin—let me see
—why that's the one that headed the band when they
stole the muskets and pewter plates from the American
army wagons. My brother was with the scouts that
pursued them. They took with them a rich booty that
time. Among other things, my brother said they had a
solid silver stand, which it was thought they had stolen
from an English officer. The scouts got pretty close to
them, and many shots were exchanged as they caught
glimpses of each other among the rocks and bushes.
One of the robbers was shot in the glens of the Clove,
and they say was never buried. The last time I heard
from there, his white bones still lay glistening among
the rocks. The muskets and plates it is thought were
hid in one of their secret caves in the Clove, but the
stand was no doubt sunk in a spring in the vicinity."

" This murder of Major Strong," said the man with
the lapstone hat, breaking in as soon as the latter
speaker paused to take a pinch of snuff, " This murder
of Major Strong was what put a stop to them."

" Have you heard the particulars of the capture of
Claudius?" interrupted the man with the frightened
voice.

" Yes; you know Major Strong was a pretty popular
man, and his murder began to make the authorities
wake up a little. The Assembly of the State took
action on the subject, and on the 31st of last month, according to their resolution, Gov. Clinton came out with
a proclamation, declaring Smith and his sons outlaws,
and offering a reward of $1200 for the capture of Clau-
dius, and $600 each for his sons Richard and James·

This was just the thing. The chance for getting money inspired many with a sudden zeal for the apprehension of the robbers, who had hitherto been indifferent about it. Claudius was a cunning dog, and knew the effect money would have on the cupidity of many, and perhaps on some of his own gang; so he fled to New York, and from there went to a secret retreat on Long Island. Among other Whig families who moved to Connecticut when the British took possession of the Island, was a wealthy farmer—John Brush. He left his landed property in the care of tenants, once in a while secretly visiting the Island to see that it was taken care of properly. While there he accidentally found out that Claudius Smith was in the same neighborhood. He knew of the rewards offered for his arrest, so he immediately went over to Connecticut and informed a friend of his, one Titus. Titus was a large, powerful, resolute man, and just the one for such an undertaking. Procuring the services of three other men, one dark night, armed with muskets and pistols, they crossed the sound in a whale boat and landed in a small bay that puts into the Island. Hauling the boat up on the sand they left it in charge of one of their number, and the rest proceeded to the house (a tavern) about a mile distant, where Smith was putting up. A light was burning, and the party entered noiselessly. The landlady, who knew Major Brush, was sitting before the fire. Brush asked her if Claudius Smith was in the house. After a short pause she replied :

"'He is in bed. I will go and call him.'

"'No; tell me where he lodges,' said Brush.

" 'Up stairs in the bedroom.'

" Warning her to keep quiet, he took a candle, and leaving one to guard her, the other three crept silently

up stairs. Without noise they slipped into the bedroom, the door of which was standing ajar, and before
he awoke seized him. He made a powerful resistance,
taken unawares as he was, and tried hard to get hold of
the pistols under his pillow, but it was useless. They
quickly tied him with a cord, and the next morning had
him safely landed in Connecticut. Brush immediately
sent a messenger to Gov. Clinton, then at Poughkeepsie,
who directed him to be brought to Fishkill. Here, as
we all know, he was taken charge of by Col. Isaac
Nicoll, the Sheriff of Orange county, and brought to
Goshen under guard of Col. Woodhull's troop of light
horse, accompanied by the leading men of the county.
And there he is now, chained to the floor, and guarded
as I said before."

" Well," said the landlord, glancing at the clock in the
corner, and yawning as he spoke, " I guess we have
about concluded Claudius' history for to-night, as I see
it's time to close. It has been pretty nearly all gone
over and summed up; all it needs now is an account of
his execution to complete it, and that I don't think we
shall have to wait for longer than the first sitting of the
court."

Here the man with the timid voice rose and said that
as he wanted a little something to strengthen his lungs,
he would propose that the man who wore the lapstone
hat should treat the company, as he was the only man
whose hat would stand a wetting. To this the owner of
the hat demurred, but finally agreed to pass it around,
which was done, and each one putting in a piece of
change the landlord treated the company for its con-
tents, and in a short time thereafter the last customer
had departed, and " Old Greycourt " was alone with its
occupants.

Well indeed had Claudius Smith been termed "The Scourge of the Highlands." Of English parentage, it was no wonder he should be inclined to adopt the creed of the mother country, and when to the principles of a rank Tory he added those of the blackest villainy and most bloodthirsty revenge, at the head of a savage crew, and in the fastnesses and caves of the Highlands, Bellvale and Warwick mountains, well and truly did he make himself so feared and dreaded as to earn the title of "The Scourge of the Highlands." His thievish propensity was said to have been encouraged by his parents, and the first article stolen, a pair of iron wedges. This talent he nursed and fostered in himself and his three sons, Richard, James, and William, and carried on on the largest scale, including occasionally the murder of some unoffending patriot of the Whig persuasion, until at last, as we have seen, he was apprehended and lodged in prison. At the January term of the court, next after his arrest, he was indicted on three or four charges of robbery and murder, and found guilty on them all. When asked by the Judge if he had anything to say in his defense, he replied with the same firmness that had characterized him all through his imprisonment and trial, "No, if God Almighty can't change your hearts I can't." The court then sentenced him and five others of his gang also found guilty at the same time, (a woman named Amy Augor or Amy Jones, Mathew Dolson, John Ryan, Thomas Delamer, and James Gordon,) to be hanged on Friday, the 22d day of January, 1779. He lived in hopes every day that his men would undertake his rescue, but he was too strongly guarded night and day for such an attempt to succeed. The day of his execution at last arrived, and with two of his men, Delamer and Gordon, he was taken from the jail to the

9

gallows. He was a large, muscular man, and walked up the steps of the scaffold with a firm, manly air. He had dressed himself with scrupulous neatness in a suit of rich broadcloth with silver buttons, and as he stood upon the scaffold and cast his eye over the assembled thousands who had gathered out of curiosity to see the great bandit die, he smiled grimly and bowed to several he knew in the crowd. It was a wild scene the clear sun shone on that winter's day in Goshen. The condemned, standing on the verge of eternity, in gorgeous apparel, with his silver buttons glittering gaily in the sunbeams, and the horde of eager thousands trampling the crisp snow, and jostling, and crowding each other for a sight of him. A man elbowed his way near the scaffold, and asked Smith to tell him where he could find his deeds and papers that were stolen from him on a certain occasion. He replied, "Mr. Youngs, this is no time to talk about papers: meet me in the next world and I'll tell you all about them." He then kicked off his shoes, saying, "My mother said I would die like a trooper's horse, with my shoes on. I will make her a false prophet and a liar." He then glanced at the eastern hills, toward the scenes of his many daring deeds, expecting, perhaps, to see his followers swooping down to his rescue from their mountain fastnesses. but they were not to be seen ; nothing met his eye but the undulating hills, covered with the crusted snow and sparkling in the sunbeams.

"That bright dream was his last."

The cap was drawn over his eyes, the rope adjusted around his neck, the cart driven from under him, and "The Scourge of the Highlands" was no more.

After the death of Claudius, his son Richard took command of the gang, the oldest son, William, having been killed in some marauding expedition the fall previous. They threatened the most dire vengeance for the hanging of their leader and the shooting of William, against every one favoring the rebel cause. On the 26th of March (1779) following they took John Clark from his residence, near the Sterling Iron Works, a piece into the woods, and after stripping off his outer garments told him to go home. While returning, with his back to them, they shot him dead and left him stretched upon a rock within sight of his dwelling. A note was left pinned to his coat, of which the following is a copy:

"A WARNING TO THE REBELS.—You are hereby warned at your peril to desist from hanging any more friends to government as you did Claudius Smith: You are warned likewise to use James Smith, James Fluelling and William Cole well, and ease them of their irons, for we are determined to have six for one, for the blood of the innocent cries aloud for vengeance. Your noted friend, Capt. Williams, and his crew of robbers and murderers we have got in our power, and the blood of Claudius Smith shall be repaid. There are particular companies of us who belong to Col. Butler's army, Indians as well as white men, and particularly numbers from New York that are resolved to be avenged on you for your cruelty and murder. We are to remind you that you are the beginners and aggressors, for by your cruel oppressions and bloody actions you drive us to it. This is the first, and we are determined to pursue it on your heads and leaders until the last—until the whole of you are murdered."

This created quite an alarm for a time, but the issuing of such rude, blustering threats soon grew to be regarded as a symptom of weakness. Their atrocities

produced here and there a man, who devoted his whole
time in following their trails and picking them off as
occasion offered. Benjamin Kelley, one of their best
men, was shortly after shot by a rebel scout named
June, who surprised them at card playing. They all
made off at the time; but Kelly's body was afterward
found near a sulphur spring where he had crawled, by
one John Henley and his dog. Claudius' sons did not
possess the talent and sagacity of their father; the
band got dissatisfied and broken up speedily under
their leadership, and at last the remaining members
were forced to flee to Canada; and thus ended the
highwayman's profession in Orange county, at least on
a large scale, it is to be hoped forever. The scene of
their exploits has changed somewhat, since those days
of lawlessness and bloodshed, but most of the localities
will long be remembered in connection with the men
that made them famous. Their retreats in the mountains can be easily found to this day by the curious,
especially the most noted, a little east of the Augusta
Iron Works in the town of Monroe. That they buried
much valuable property in these mountains, may be
inferred from the fact that in 1805 or 1806, some of
Smith's descendants came from Canada, and searched
for the property according to the directions that had
been handed down to them. They found a lot of muskets in a good state of preservation, but nothing else.
Again, about 1824, two men, descendants of Edward
Roblin, came from Canada with written directions, and
explored the country thoroughly but found nothing.
Various other persons fished in the spring where it was
said the silver stand was sunk, but without success;
and it is generally supposed that some member of the
band found out the depository, unknown to Smith or

Roblin, and appropriated it to his own use. At any rate, there is no record of the treasures ever having been found, and unless revealed by chance, it will most probably remain entombed till the sound of the last trump, if it has not been recently removed.

Well may those days be called "the times that tried men's souls," judging from the glimpse we have taken at a small period in the history of Orange, and a few instances only of Tory robbery, cruelty and murder, such as marked the history of Claudius Smith and his men. Thanks to Providence we shall never see the like again.

CHAPTER XV.

The stream that forms the subject of this sketch, is composed of two principal branches, both of which rise in the town of Chester. The one rising in the west, is first known as Meadow brook, and flows northwardly into the town of Goshen, assuming as it becomes enlarged the title of Otterkill. The one rising in the east goes by the cognomen of Trout brook for a short distance, and then by that of Seely's creek, till it flows through the Greycourt meadows, after which it is called by some Greycourt creek, and by others the Cromline creek, in honor of Daniel Cromline, one of the first settlers in the vicinity, and the founder of " Greycourt Inn." It flows northwardly to near the boundary line between the towns of Hamptonburgh and Blooming Grove, where it unites with the Otterkill at a small village of the same name. After the junction of the two streams the continuance is known as Murderer's creek, and flows through portions of the towns of Blooming Grove, Cornwall and New Windsor, finally emptying into the Hudson river between Cornwall Landing and the village of New Windsor, at Plum Point, the village at its mouth being known as Moodna.

A century and a half ago, as the tradition goes, long years before the wilderness that lined its banks and furnished a home for the wild beast and Indian, had given way to the busy industry of the white man; long before the mills, and factories, and beautiful villages that now throng its shores had an existence in the dreams of either the red or white man, its surrounding wilds were inhabited by a tribe of Indians whose name, like themselves, has long since been buried in oblivion. Here the smoke of their wigwams rose in graceful wreaths upon the still summer air, amid the shouts of the young braves, who sported, as perhaps their race had done for centuries beneath the shade of their native oaks, unaware that destiny had doomed them to ultimate extinction, and their hunting grounds to the possession of a superior race. Yes, unaware that even then the forerunner of the coming tide that was to overwhelm them, was marching toward them with gigantic strides. It soon became known to them that a different race of beings were arriving along the shores of the great river that flowed past them to the ocean, but though at first much alarmed at the sight of them, they soon found them to be mortal like themselves, and at length grew to utterly disregard them. At last a white man named Martelair came and asked permission to build a house and to live near the mouth of their beautiful creek. This they readily granted, and in a very short time he constructed a log house about three or four hundred yards up the creek. Into this he soon moved his family, consisting of his wife and two children, one a boy of five, and the other a girl of three years old. He understood the importance of being on friendly terms with his rude neighbors, and made himself useful to them by a variety of acts highly estimated among savage tribes. He

never lost an opportunity of proving his good will
toward them by making them accept his hospitality,
and his house became a place of general resort. An
old Indian called Naoman, was in particular very friendly, and would often come and sit in the house for hours,
and smoke and play with the children. But Martelair
heard of the difficulties in other sections between the
settlers and Indians, and knew that his neighbors might
prove treacherous at any moment. He discovered an
island, some distance down the Hudson, which was well
adapted as a place of refuge, and could be easily defended with a little preparation. When absent from
home and unobserved, he arranged a small place among
the rocks on this island so that one or two could defend
it against an overwhelming force, and to this he resolved
to flee in case of danger.

One day, when Martelair was absent, old Naoman
came to his house, and as usual lighted his pipe and sat
down. But it was easy to see that he was troubled
about something, for his face wore a serious look, and
every little while he would shake his head and sigh
deeply, though he said not a word. Martelair's wife
asked him what was the matter, but he made no reply
and soon went away. He came the next day, and again
went away in the same manner as before. Martelair's
wife related his strange behavior to her husband, and
he told her to urge the old Indian to tell her the cause
if he came again. He came the next day, and Martelair's wife at once insisted on knowing the cause of his
trouble. She was so importunate that at last Naoman
said:

"I am a red man, and the pale faces are our enemies;
why should I speak?"

"But," said Martelair's wife. "my husband and I are

your friends; you have eaten salt with us a hundred times, and my children have often sat on your knees. If you have anything on your mind, tell it to me; perhaps we can help you."

" If it is found out, it will cost me my life, and the pale faced women are not good at keeping secrets," replied the old man.

" Try me and see."

" Will you swear by the great spirit to tell none but your husband ?"

" I have no one else to tell."

" But will you swear ?"

" I do swear by the great spirit," said Martelair's wife, " that I will tell none but my husband."

" Not if my tribe should kill you for not telling ?"

" Not if your tribe should kill me for not telling."

This satisfied the old Indian, and he then told her that his tribe had become so angry at the doings of the settlers below the mountains, that they were resolved that very night to massacre all the pale faces within their reach. That if she would escape she must inform her husband speedily, take to their boat and seek a place of safety before nightfall. And above all to excite no suspicion if possible. Naoman then departed, and the wife at once sought her husband. He was out on the river fishing. She called him to the shore and told him the dread intelligence. No time was to be lost, and he at once sprang from the canoe and sought his boat. It was partly filled with water and some time was consumed in bailing it out. When it was finished and his wife and children seated in it, Martelair bethought him of his gun which was in the house. This he went back after, of course occupying a little time— oh ! how precious, as it afterward proved. As he pulled

9*

off from the shore, he did not notice the solitary Indian who was observing every motion from the hillside. The frequent visits of Naoman to Martelair's family had aroused the suspicions of the tribe, and a watch had been kept upon their movements. This was the business of the Indian on the hillside, and when he saw them going down the river in the boat, he at once ran to the village and gave the alarm. Five stalwart chiefs at once ran down to the edge of the river, jumped into their canoes and paddled swiftly after Martelair, who had already gained a considerable distance. He saw them coming and strained every nerve to escape. The boat quivered as it cleft the dancing waves in headlong speed, obedient to the sturdy strokes of the oars, and left a trail of crested foam behind. But Martelair saw that his pursuers were gaining on him rapidly in spite of his efforts. Twice he dropped his oars and drew his rifle to fire upon them, but his wife each time grasped his arm, telling him if he fired and should after all be overtaken, they would be sure to obtain no mercy. He refrained each time, and again bent to the oars with the energy of despair. His island refuge was in sight; if he could succeed in gaining it he would bid defiance to the whole tribe until some passing sloop or ship would relieve him. The strength of his strokes almost caused the boat to bound from the water. Great drops of sweat rolled from his forehead as he plied the oars on that race for the lives of himself, his weeping wife and children. But it was all in vain. He was overtaken within a hundred yards of the island shore, and taken back with yells of triumph. (This island is opposite West Point, was partly fortified by the Americans in 1775, and is still known as " Martelair's Rock Island.") After reaching the shore with their prisoners, the Indians set fire to Martelair's house, and proceeded to the village with their captives. A council was immediately convened to determine their fate. This was composed of the chief men of the tribe, among them old Naoman. The principal brave stated that some of the tribe had proved treacherous and informed the pale faces of the designs of the tribe. He proposed that the prisoners should be examined in regard to it. This was agreed to, and an Indian who could talk English acted as interpreter. Martelair was questioned first, but resolutely refused to reveal his informant. His wife was questioned next, while to terrify her two Indians stood with drawn tomahawks threatening the two children. She told them that she had a frightful dream the night before and had persuaded her husband to fly.

"The Great Spirit never deigns to talk in dreams to a pale face," said the chief. "Woman, thou hast two tongues and two faces; speak the truth, or thy children shall surely die." The little boy and girl were then placed beside her, and the two savages stood by with drawn weapons to execute his orders.

"Will you name," said the chief, "the traitor who betrayed his tribe? I will ask three times."

The mother was pale and trembling, but did not answer.

"Will you name him?" said the chief. "This is the second time."

The tears gathered in the mother's eyes as she glanced at her husband and children. She stole a glance at Naoman, but the old chief was smoking as unconcernedly as though ignorant of their presence. She wrung her hands in silent agony but answered not a word.

"Again," said the chief, "will you name the traitor? This is the third time."

The agony of the mother's mind was fearful. Bitter tears ran down her cheeks. The tomahawks were raised over the heads of the children for the death blow, and their voices were united in frightful cries for their mother to save them. She again glanced through her tears at Naoman, but his eye was as cold and indifferent as before. Still she kept her word. Another moment would be her children's last.

Suddenly Naoman rose to his feet. All paused and turned their eyes toward him. " Stop !" he cried with a tone of authority as he drew his majestic form to its fullest hight; " The pale faced woman has kept her pledge. Braves, I am the traitor. I ate of the salt, warmed myself at the fire, played with the children, enjoyed the kindness of the pale faced Christians, and it was I who warned them of their danger. Braves, for many moons I have been your companion on the war path. I am old and useless in the war dance. I am a withered, leafless, branchless trunk; cut me down if you will, I am ready; but never let it be said that old Naoman forgot his friends." The old Indian's remarks were followed for a moment with perfect silence, but the Indian character could not appreciate the motives of his course; the next instant a yell of indignation arose from all sides. The old chief stepped down from the bank whereon he had been sitting, and covered his face with his mantle of skins; the next moment a tomahawk cleft his skull and he fell dead at the feet of those he had so nobly died to save.

" But the sacrifice of Naoman," says Paulding, " and the firmness of the Christian white woman, did not suffice to save the lives of the other victims. They perished—how, it is needless to say."

Many years have passed since then. The murdered

and the murderers have long ago gone to meet their
reward in the spirit land.   Splendid farms and happy
homes now occupy the scene of the tragic incidents
attending the death of Martelair's family.   But the
memory of their fate has survived the lapse of time, and
is still preserved by the name of the pleasant stream
on whose banks they lived and died, which, to this day,
is called Murderer's creek.

CHAPTER XVI.

Sluggishly the current of the Wallkill was rolling along one afternoon not many weeks ago. The morning had possessed all the requisites deemed so necessary to success in fishing as well as hunting,

"A southerly wind and a cloudy sky;"

but though I occupied about the best fishing ground along the stream, (a few miles above Pellet's Island bridge), had changed my base of operations many times, and had "cast my lines" in many pleasant places during the day, still the array of fish in my basket continued alarmingly small. At last scarce a nibble disturbed the serene repose of my line in the deep water, and allowing the end of my pole to drop in after the line, I leaned back on the rank wild grass that covered the bank, drew my hat over my eyes to keep off the glare of the sun that had just broke through the scattering clouds, and naturally enough, my thoughts recurred to the reminiscences that cluster around the vicinity of the gliding stream before me. How many a swift canoe had darted over its surface and followed its crooked course, rounding the bends with a graceful curve, obedient to the command of some stalwart Indi-

an chief. How many a dark female of the woods, in
all the regal beauty of her native wildness, had roamed
along its banks, and had perhaps been wooed and won
beside the sparkling water and beneath the overhanging
boughs of the leafy maple and water birch, that then
no doubt, presented an interminable forest on either
side. Yes! and how many scenes of strife, and daring
strategy, and wild ventures for life, and narrow escapes
it had witnessed in the days when the bear, panther,
wolf and red man mutually came from the dark recesses
of their native fastnesses to bathe in and drink its
limpid flood, long years before the white man and his
attendant, civilization, had made themselves known in
these mighty solitudes, where the Indian· had indeed
sought and found a home.

> "Some safer world in depth of wood embrac'd,
> Some happier island in the wat'ry waste,
> Where slaves once more their native land behold,
> No fiends torment, no Christians thirst for gold."

And, since the advent of civilization, how many companies of gay ladies and gentlemen had sailed over its
surface, had discoursed with grammatical precision, had
fished with all the ease and grace polite society confers,
had flirted in the most approved style, and in all the
pride of good looks that the most profuse use of paint
could produce and the dignity of garments of the most
fashionable make inspire; on the very spot perhaps
where hundreds of years before the Indian wooed his
dusky maid in all the simplicity of savage wildness,
with no paint but the war paint that decked his every
limb, in garments that had never felt the snip of shears
or hiss of tailor's goose, and in language that can scarce
be said to have a grammar. Yet death has sent them
to mingle in one circle in the happy spirit land—either

the "civilized" stripped of their pride, hypocrisy, art
and science, or the savage at once put in possession of
all these faculties by the hand of omnipotent power.

Many a social revel, in a friendly way, of hardy hands
and honest hearts, and many a day of pure enjoyment,
too, has this old stream seen. Happy days of fishing in
the pleasant fall and summer months, and lucky days of
hunting in the early spring, when the " drowned lands"
are overflowed with melting snow and the spring rains
for the distance of a mile or more on either side, and
the wild duck and goose make it their home. Days of
enjoyment too, that will cause it to be long remembered,
as well alike by the pretty country maiden who has
roamed along its side, as by the hard fisted farmer who
frequented it to find respite from his daily toil. And
there are other mementos of it that recall to mind sad
and painful thoughts. It was near this spot not many
years ago, that a young man in springing from a boat
in which were a number of ladies who had been upon a
pleasure excursion, fell short of the shore and sank to
rise no more in sight of his horrified companions. Only
a few miles below here, and but a year or so ago, the
lamented young Dr. Putney was drowned by the acci-
dental upsetting of his canoe while out hunting. And
well do I remember hearing old residents of the vicinity
tell the particulars of another sad incident, which now
occurs to my mind.

In the spring of the year 1827, the freshet upon the
"drowned lands" was unusually high. The geese and
ducks were holding high carnival on its wide extended
surface and amid its submerged swamps. Duck shooting occupied the minds of all who were in the habit of
taking an occasional holiday in that kind of amusement,
or who had any relish for a bit of roast game now and

then. The morning of the 15th of March of that year dawned exceedingly blustery and cold, but it did not deter two young men from leaving home to engage in a day's hunting along the Wallkill. They had their minds made up a day or so before, and were determined to let no trivial circumstance disappoint them of a day's sport. One of them left a young and beautiful wife— a lady who attracted attention wherever she appeared by her handsome looks and imperial manner; in fact was the admired and envied of a large circle of acquaintances surrounding the then thriving little village of Brookfield. The other was unmarried. Both were men of good families and extensively known. The day passed away and they did not return. Another dragged its slow length along to the now alarmed and anxious families awaiting them, and still they did not come. Ah! look, young wife, through the long, long day, and sleepless, lonesome night, and mourn; and you, too, ye friends, for they never shall return in the pride of their strength and manhood. Their well known manly forms shall never again occupy their former places in the family circle. Never more shall their vivacious conversation, their ever ready jest, or their merry ringing laugh be heard this side the grave. For the unpitying waters of the Wallkill have taken them to its deadly embrace, and buried in eternal stillness the flow of their genial souls on earth.

How they struggled for life no mortal man may know. What agonized and frenzied feelings wrought their breasts in those long hours of suffering, no pen can ever tell, when after the upsetting of their canoe they found themselves so benumbed by cold and wet as to be unable to get it righted, and were forced at last to abandon it and make a last venture for life and the mainland. The water not being very deep here, in some places in reality of easy wading depth, (it was some distance from the main channel,) they struggled on through sunken morasses and dangerous quagmires with the desperation of despair. Alternately buoyed up with a faint hope, and anon hopeless, as obstacles were overcome and stronger ones came to view, till at last fatigue and cold crowded out the little spark of life, and they perished in sight of the dry land for which they were striving. The searching parties shortly after found them and dragged ashore the remains of these two unfortunate men, and many is the time the hard fate of Duncan Hulse and Milton Howell has been told around the evening fireside by those to whose memory it is as a tale of yesterday.

Years have passed since then, and time, as ever, has wrought its changes. Not long since I was standing in the streets of a neighboring village, when I chanced to notice a wasted female form passing by. Her faded calico dress was fluttering in the breeze like the last sere leaves of autumn that still cling trembling to the trees. A bonnet of straw that had apparently been bleached by the sun of many summers, with a single flower and bow-knot of the same faded hue adorning the top, completed her attire. Onward she passed with trembling hand and wild maniacal stare, with head ever shaking, shaking, and incoherent sentences constantly issuing from her lips. The boys stopped their play for a moment as she went by, and said, " Poor crazy Betsy." Yes, this was the once accomplished and beautiful bride, the admired and envied wife.

The waters of the Wallkill are still noiselessly gliding on,

"Onward, ever onward, and still on to the sea,"

unmindful of the incidents time brings beside its shores.
Even so—

> " Life is a stream—how fair its face,
>   How smooth its dimpling waters pace,
>   Its canopy how pure.
>   But rocks below, and tempests sleep,
>   Insidious o'er the glassy deep,
>   Nor leave an hour secure."

Yes, reader, such is life, and before many years you and
I will disappear beneath its surface and be known on
earth no more.   But never mind,

> "My friend, adown life's valley, hand in hand,
>   With grateful change of grave and merry speech,
>   Or song, our hearts unlocking each to each,
>   We'll journey onward to the silent land."

THE END.

www.ingramcontent.com/pod-product-compliance
Lightning Source LLC
Chambersburg PA
CBHW020613030726
47497CB00007B/2219